The Handbook of Facilities Management

In today's dynamic and complex business environment, integrated facilities management has become an essential function for organizations navigating decentralized and often overlooked departments across multiple real estate properties and diverse geographical locations.

The demand for a cohesive and strategic approach to construction, facilities management, finance, real estate, and the supply chain, has shifted from being merely advantageous to being a critical necessity. Such an approach mitigates risk, optimizes resources, and enhances cost efficiency. This book is relevant to all enterprises in every industry, but it continually highlights the healthcare industry because that environment is arguably the best example of the complexity, challenges, and pressures in creating and maintaining facilities management unity.

The premise of the book presents facilities management practices as the rule rather than the exception, and details how disjointed operations, uncoordinated vendor management, and insufficient oversight can lead to inefficiencies, increased organizational risk, and potential threats to continuity and financial performance. Given this, the author offers operational, managerial, and technological solutions for the reader.

The Handbook of Facilities Management

A Guide to Integrated Excellence

Steve F. Sawyer

Routledge
Taylor & Francis Group
A PRODUCTIVITY PRESS BOOK

Designed cover image: Shutterstock

First published 2027
by Routledge
605 Third Avenue, New York, NY 10158

and by Routledge
4 Park Square, Milton Park, Abingdon, Oxon, OX14 4RN

Routledge is an imprint of the Taylor & Francis Group, an informa business

ISBN: 9781041303268 (hbk)
ISBN: 9781041303251 (pbk)
ISBN: 9781003773955 (ebk)

DOI: 10.4324/9781003773955

Typeset in Garamond
by Newgen Publishing UK

To my wife: my best friend, my constant supporter, and a 12-year cancer survivor whose strength amazes me every day. To our three children, who remind me what truly matters, and to my parents, grandparents, family, and mentors—your wisdom and encouragement have guided every step of my journey. This book exists because of all of you.

Contents

Author Biography

Steve F. Sawyer is an executive with diverse experience in transforming integrated facilities management, commercial real estate, and global supply chain operations for Fortune 500 and private sector companies. He has a proven track record aligning multi-billion-dollar procurement, capital planning, and vendor strategies to deliver substantial cost savings and operational efficiencies.

Since 2020 he has been Executive Vice President-Operations and Technology for SolvingX, LLC, which provides technology and operational solutions in global supply chain, integrated facilities management.

He has held executive leadership positions in major facilities, supply chain, and real estate industry companies, including:

- Jones, Lang Lasalle, Inc. (JLL), a global real estate services company with offices in 80 countries, where he served as Vice President, Sourcing and Procurement for the Americas in both Category Management and Facilities & Real Estate Operations. He led efforts to develop and integrate 25 global business systems with a combined $16 billion in capital, construction, direct, indirect, and trailing spend.

- CBRE Inc., a Fortune 500 global facilities and real estate management company. Serving as Director of Strategic Sourcing, he directed the $180 million Americas spend, involving 150 hospitals and more than 3,000 non-hospital facilities totaling 25 million square feet.
- Premier Inc., the second largest healthcare-focused group purchasing organization (GPO) in the United States. As Director of Strategic Sourcing (Construction, Energy, Environmental Services, and Facilities), he led a $1 billion, 50-category sourcing portfolio—driving 20% growth in vendor spend and contract utilization ($790,000,000 to $1billion) while ensuring full compliance across all sourcing activities.

Steve is a member of the Johnson Controls Healthcare Advisory Council for 2025 representing the Energy-as-a-Service, Fire/Life Safety, HVAC, & Securities sectors. Sitelink. He is also a 2025 Board Member for Sitelink, representing the Digital Twin and Building Information Modeling tech integrated with Augmented Reality sectors.

With a coach-to-player leadership philosophy, is adept at building high-performing teams across healthcare, banking, retail, data centers, government, and real estate investment trust sectors.

- Midwest Regional Manager for the Duke Energy account, providing direct oversight of 3.5 million sq. ft. of mixed office space and operation center support facilities.

Foreword: Strategic Leadership in Facilities Management—A Call for Integrated, Purpose-Driven Practice

David R. Doxsey

Over the course of my 30-year professional journey, I have come to recognize that the role of facilities management—across commercial, healthcare, and manufacturing sectors—extends far beyond the upkeep of physical infrastructure. It is about shaping environments where healing, precision, and productivity are not simply preferred—they are essential. The environments we maintain directly influence patient outcomes, operational effectiveness, and the lived experiences of those who deliver care and drive progress.

What continues to inspire me is the extraordinary transformation of this field. Facilities management has evolved from a behind-the-scenes function into a central driver of institutional strategy and enterprise resilience. Today, facility leaders are no longer defined solely by operational oversight; they are integrators, trusted advisors, and stewards of long-term value who contribute meaningfully to the future of care, innovation, and organizational excellence.

With this evolution comes a greater responsibility—one rooted not just in execution, but in collaboration, humility, and trust. Operational competence remains foundational, but leadership in today's landscape requires cross-functional fluency. Facilities professionals must now collaborate deliberately and continuously with partners across Construction, Finance, Information Technology, Real Estate, and Supply Chain. These functions, once considered parallel, have become inseparable. Together, they support the performance and resilience of the organization as a whole.

Crucially, this type of multidisciplinary collaboration is not traditionally taught in academic programs. Rather, it is learned through experience—through the nuanced realities of enterprise operations, and through what I have come to regard as the **A–Z of Strategic Facilities Management**:

A – Asset Optimization
Enhancing asset value through proactive maintenance, lifecycle planning, and data-informed decisions.

B – Budget Alignment
Ensuring operational priorities and capital strategies are reflected in financial planning.

C – Capital Planning
Strategically allocating resources for infrastructure, modernization, and long-term improvements.

D – Data-Driven Decision-Making
Utilizing analytics to forecast needs, assess performance, and guide investment.

E – Energy Management
Advancing efficiency and sustainability through reduced consumption and carbon initiatives.

F – Facility Compliance
Adhering to all regulatory frameworks to ensure safety, continuity, and readiness.

G – Governance Frameworks
Establishing clear accountability, protocols, and operational standards across teams.

H – Health & Safety Protocols
Maintaining environments that protect patients, staff, and visitors alike.

I – Integrated Technology Systems
Leveraging smart building tools, IoT, and CMMS platforms to modernize operations.

J – Joint Commission Readiness
Sustaining compliance in clinical settings to ensure accreditation and safety.

K – Knowledge Transfer
Preserving institutional wisdom through documentation, mentorship, and cross-training.

L – Lifecycle Costing
Evaluating total cost of ownership to guide investment and resource use.

M – Maintenance Strategy
Balancing preventive, predictive, and corrective tactics to maximize uptime and longevity.

N – Net-Zero Planning
Developing facilities-led pathways to decarbonization and environmental leadership.

O – Organizational Change Management
Leading teams through system, space, and cultural transitions with clarity and care.

P – Project Delivery

Executing upgrades and new builds with precision and minimal disruption.

Q – Quality Assurance

Applying rigorous standards to ensure consistent performance and reliability.

R – Regulatory Compliance

Meeting or exceeding evolving legal, environmental, and safety mandates.

S – Strategic Sourcing

Building values-aligned partnerships that advance quality, sustainability, and agility.

T – Talent Development

Fostering growth, certification, and leadership within facility teams.

U – Utility Resilience

Safeguarding continuity of power, water, HVAC, and other essential services.

V – Vendor Management

Holding external partners accountable through KPIs, contracts, and performance metrics.

W – Workplace Strategy

Designing adaptive, human-centered environments that align with organizational priorities.

X – Cross-Functional Execution

Bridging departmental silos to enable integrated outcomes across the enterprise.

Y – Yield Improvement

Refining processes to enhance facility output, throughput, or cost efficiency.

Z – Zero Harm Culture

Embedding safety-first values into every facet of operations and leadership.

The "facilities badge," I believe, is earned not through title, but through presence—by consistently listening to frontline teams, responding with agility, and demonstrating reliability, credibility, and empathy. The most effective leaders in this space lead not by authority, but by example.

High-performing organizations understand that facilities are not just physical assets—they are strategic systems, essential to long-term success. Today, facilities management is central to achieving institutional missions—whether through capital planning, environmental stewardship, or digital transformation. Facility leaders must therefore be equipped to think both operationally and strategically, bridging the gap between systems performance and enterprise vision.

Technology and analytics have accelerated this evolution. These tools allow us to uncover inefficiencies, mitigate risk, and direct smarter investments. Yet, they are not a substitute for leadership. What truly distinguishes resilient organizations is the ability to translate insight into action through trusted, cross-functional partnerships.

Strategic sourcing, once narrowly viewed as procurement, has evolved into a value-driven practice built on shared accountability and aligned vision. Similarly, project execution today demands rigor, governance, and a focus on disruption mitigation. Outsourcing, when thoughtfully governed, provides the agility and expertise to remain responsive to shifting priorities and operational complexity.

At the core of all these efforts are people—particularly the Facility Engineers and operations teams whose knowledge, precision, and dedication ensure that spaces remain safe, functional, and aligned with purpose. Their insights are indispensable. Their contributions are invaluable. And their leadership must be recognized and supported.

This book captures the full breadth of what modern facilities management requires. It is more than a compilation of best practices—it is a strategic guide shaped by humility, collaboration, and earned experience. It reminds us that this profession is as much about people and purpose as it is about process and performance.

As I reflect on the insights shared within these pages, I am reminded that we are not simply managing buildings—we are safeguarding the environments where care is delivered, innovation is cultivated, and lives are transformed. It is a profound responsibility, and a privilege to carry it.

I am honored to endorse this publication. It serves as a valuable resource for facility professionals, executives, and emerging leaders alike. May it encourage thoughtful leadership, strengthen collaborative culture, and reinforce our collective commitment to environments that rise to meet the mission—every single day.

David R. Doxsey

David R. Doxsey is the Senior Vice President of Building & Engineering for LilliBridge Healthcare Services Inc. (LHS), the wholly owned property management and leasing subsidiary of Ventas, one of the world's foremost real estate investment trusts. In this role, he is responsible for the national leadership of engineering and maintenance operations for the LHS Medical Office Building (MOB) portfolio. He develops strategies and direction to ensure delivery of superior customer services and attain financial objectives.

Acknowledgments

I sincerely acknowledge Lee Reeder—supporter, writer, and friend—who has walked alongside me throughout this new book journey. I am also deeply grateful to the invaluable mentors and interviewees who have guided me throughout my career: Andy Thompson, Carl Johnson, Curt Grantham, David Doxsey, David Jones, Jeanne Armentrout, Jim Gross, Lee Reeder, Mark Mininberg, Michael Georgulis, Pete Bulgarelli, Rick Michaux, Sandra James, and Wes Thiss—along with countless lifelong friends in facilities management, father how managed facilities, and family. Your support, wisdom, and encouragement have been instrumental to my growth and success.

Introduction

In today's dynamic and complex business environment, integrated facilities management (IFM) has become an essential function for organizations navigating decentralized and often overlooked departments across multiple real estate properties and diverse geographical locations. The demand for a cohesive and strategic approach to construction, facilities management, finance, information technology, real estate, and supply chain has shifted from being merely advantageous to being a critical necessity. Such an approach mitigates risk, optimizes resources, and enhances cost efficiency.

For senior leaders, including chief financial officers, chief operating officers, and executive or senior vice presidents tasked with overseeing these functions, the challenges of fragmented facilities management practices are well known. Disjointed operations, insufficient oversight, and uncoordinated vendor management can lead to inefficiencies, increased organizational risk, and potential threats to both operational continuity and financial performance.

This book is meant for professionals in any industry, but just to make things a little more interesting, many of my cases and examples will come from perspective of perhaps the

DOI: 10.4324/9781003773955-1

most challenging industry in facilities management, and one in which much of my experience lies. That's healthcare.

Healthcare is exceptional for many reasons. Fundamentally, it is one of the few industries that has what I call that "extra layer" of burden. In healthcare that additional layer to consider is represented by one patient, because in healthcare you live and die—every hour, every minute, every day of the week—on that one patient.

What makes it different is the regulatory environment. Different industries have varying levels of regulatory pressures, but few are under level of scrutiny that leaders in healthcare experience. So, as I provide context with examples from healthcare it may add extra layer of pressure that you might not be under in your own industry, but I believe it will take things to a little higher level.

The following is a preview of what I detail in the book:

Chapter 1 introduces the importance of creating unity across the disparate business units/departments that make up a truly integrated enterprise, providing a framework for assessing the strength of the "marriage." I outline my process for assessing an organization, including detail on key performance indicators (KPIs) to look for in each of the business units. This chapter also introduces the importance of high-quality data and having a robust role and responsibility framework.

In Chapter 2, I introduce the importance of the connection of Facilities and Supply Chain business units and how they are tied together by analytics, formal policies and procedures and their roles and responsibilities when it comes two key areas of contracting—master service agreements and service line agreements. I introduce RACI—the time-honored role clarity and accountability framework—with its elements of Responsible

Accountable, Consulted and Informed. I detail how the RACI matrix serves to create cohesion across business units.

Chapter 3 looks at how IFM business units can partner with Finance in achieving true realized savings. These elements include:

- The importance of analyzing and cleansing data.
- Real-life cases in achieving realized savings.
- Balancing budget reductions and increases in IFM.
- The effects of IFM asset management and capital planning programs on Finance.
- Right-sizing the IFM general ledger.

Chapter 4 is a comprehensive view of the foundations of an effective IFM strategy including streamlining operations for greater efficiency. The theme of self-performance—commitment to maximizing in-house capabilities over outsourcing—which is visited throughout the book, is introduced in detail in this chapter. Essential facilities-specific KPIs and associated metrics are also presented as a toolkit for readers.

Chapter 5 details the necessity of synergy between the Facilities and Supply Chain business units in IFM, specifically in collaboratively developing contracts and conducting vendor management. The nature of collaboration between Facilities and Supply Chain is explored in other areas as well, including category management, strategic sourcing, optimization, and rationalization. Supply Chain-specific KPIs and metrics are also presented. The chapter closes by introducing Group Purchasing Organizations and some of the pros and cons of working with them in IFM.

Chapter 6 combines considerations for the closely related Real Estate and Construction business units, covering several key issues, including:

- Relationships between Real Estate and Construction.
- Capital planning.
- Portfolio management.
- Property management.
- How construction innovates to meet top organizational objectives.
- Considerations in Construction repurposing a retail environment to healthcare.

In Chapter 7, I provide strategies for enhancing collaboration within IFM. This includes a vision for an "integrated facilities management collaborative" forming a pyramid in which information and collaboration continuously flows among top leadership through all of the business units/departments of the IFM enterprise. This chapter combines several key elements of collaboration, including the perils of departmental separation, methods of improving communication, handing meetings, managing stakeholders and data, and maintaining role and responsibility clarity.

Chapter 8 details how to integrate technology into IFM business units and how the methods we use to manage and use data can bond the entire IFM enterprise together. Key issues covered include:

- The role of the IT department in managing IFM enterprise technology.
- How AI can help us expose concealed costs and unlock hidden value.
- Tapping into the flood of unstructured data in IFM for improvement.
- The importance of balancing AI with human oversight.

Chapter 9 weighs the potential benefits and drawbacks of outsourcing the work of business units associated with IFM. Pros and cons of outsourcing are presented, along with tips and techniques for selecting and managing outside partners. The chapter also defines aggregators and explores the differentiators between aggregators and niche advisory firms in outsourcing for use in evaluating what kind of outsourcing model an IFM enterprise might benefit from. Finally it looks at the relation of total cost of ownership (TCO), also known as asset lifecycle management, to the decision of whether to outsource.

In Chapter 10 I bring it all together by exploring the transformation of facilities management leadership, taking a coach-to-player mentoring approach. In this chapter I pivot and bring in some valuable leadership perspective from two esteemed colleagues that I have worked with over the years:

Andrew Thompson, current COO of Dallas-based Zarmanali Pediatrics, who has also served recently as the COO of Pediatric Associates—the largest pediatric medical group in the United States, with more than 300 practices across seven states.

David J. Jones, current Regional Market President for CommonSpirit Health, with oversight of nearly 30 hospitals in several states.

Their input comes from both strategic and in-the-trenches viewpoints on issues ranging from role accountability and responsibility to methods for driving alignment and strategic vision, to breaking down organizational silos through transparency and communication.

In Chapter 11 I wrap up the book by looking at how current and anticipated changes, especially in technology, are helping to create a more truly integrated world for facilities management. I close with suggestions for bringing up and supporting the next generation of IFM leaders.

It is my hope that the principles outlined in this book inspire you to elevate your infrastructure and staff competencies, fostering a cohesive IFM approach. By strengthening partnerships and ecosystem collaboration, organizations can expand their market presence and successfully penetrate new geographies, ensuring sustained success in an increasingly competitive global landscape.

We'll first dive into it by examining facilities management in terms of a relationship.

Chapter 1

From Family Feud to Unity

Coming together is a beginning, staying together is progress, and working together is success.

–Henry Ford

Optimizing resources, enhancing cost efficiency, and mitigating risk in today's facilities management environment requires bringing together disparate departments/business units that often have a limited track record of truly working together. It requires a marriage of Finance, Real Estate, Construction, Facilities Management, Supply Chain, and Information Technology.

When I first begin working with an entity that is flirting with the notion of instituting fully integrated facilities management (IFM), I start with a single question to myself: Where does this organization lie on the scale of unity?

I start with that one question not only because it has the power to generate a flood of literally hundreds of others, but

DOI: 10.4324/9781003773955-2

also because any corporate commitment shares many of the qualities of a good (or bad) personal relationship. In those terms, every organization will fall under one of the following of what I call identity statuses:

1. *Single*: This is when the entity is completely non-integrated, operating business unit by business unit—untethered and uncommitted—resisting efforts to limit their freedom to do as they please.
2. *Dating*: Then there are those who are exploring the potential for full integration. Still, they need more data to be convinced that giving up their independence and self-determination will be worth the commitment.
3. *Married*: These organizations are doing the work and maintaining the devotion to being fully integrated across all departments/business units. A steady stream of positive data emanating from their efforts keeps them from straying from their bond.
4. *Divorced*: These organizations tried to work toward IFM but could not resist the temptation to return to the "good old days" of interdepartmental conflict and fragmentation.

Figure 1.1 presents the elements involved in determining the level of unity in integrated facilities management. How does an outsider like me figure out where an entity stands with regard to unity in facilities management?

First, I begin by thinking like an insider, armed with the Chief Operating Officer/Chief Financial Officer (COO/CFO) mindset that comes natural to me after decades of organizational assessment experience. I am usually hired by a COO into an organization that is at the Dating stage or in the throes of Divorce.

I begin with a departmental interview/assessment process that examines the following departmental/business unit areas:

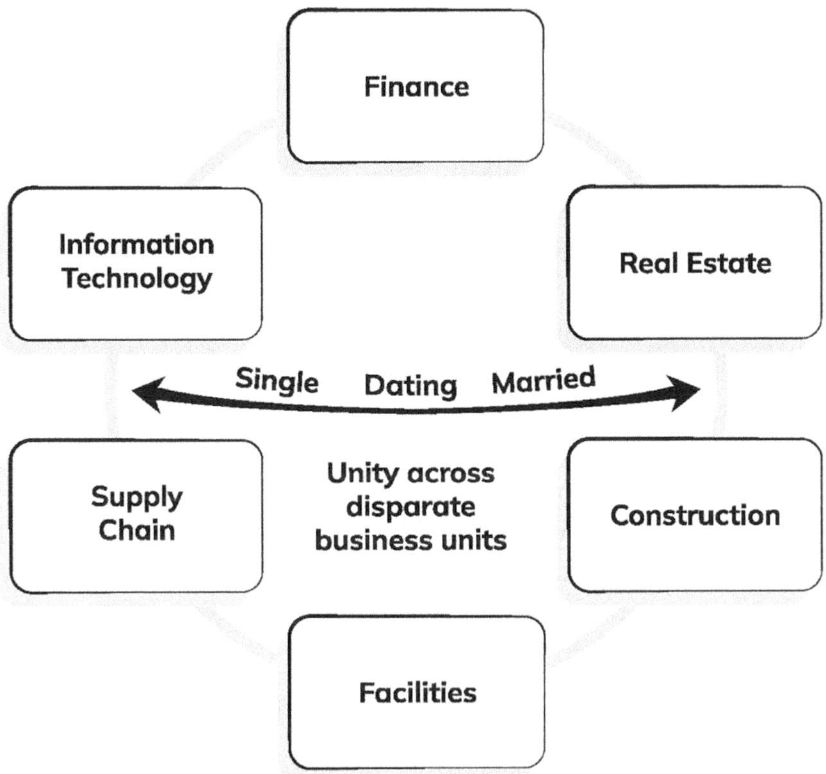

Figure 1.1 Getting to unity in integrated facilities management. (Figure content and concept created by the author.)

- Finance
- Real Estate
- Construction
- Facilities
- Supply Chain
- Information Technology

Keep in mind that not all organizations I work with at the outset will not have formally instituted all of these separate departments/business units. This is due to a number of reasons, including their size, outsourcing some units, or combining/sharing certain responsibilities among various units. Still, my assessment follows this logic of six distinct areas of responsibility in the scheme of IFM.

By the time I begin talking with the principals in each of these areas, I have done a fair amount of upfront homework on the organizational structure, so I know the departments I am walking into and who is managing them. Only after I have examined that data in detail to get the lay of the land will I begin my interview process.

It starts with a corporate executive introducing me to the principals so they can be assured that this effort has the full endorsement of top c-suite management.

Remember that my ultimate goal is to create a truly integrated IFM program, but my overarching question at first is where this entire organization is currently sitting when it comes to unity. I am ever mindful that the nature of the questions I have to ask in this process may be intimidating to the managers in these business units.

Whether you are an outside consultant like me or an inside COO or other executive trying to create facilities management transformation, you need to clear the air right up front about your motives. This is especially critical for organizations in which siloed departments and turf wars have long dominated. In these entities any comprehensive examination will have the managers flinching from the assumption that their business unit is about to be *riffed* (experience a reduction in force) as a result of your work.

Their fears are well-founded. Any seasoned manager in a facilities-related department knows that when representatives from a major IFM service provider come into an organization, one of the main tools in their toolbox, figuratively speaking, is a scythe. That's because their business model demands the Reduction in force (RIF); reducing the workforce and partially supplanting it is how they make a good percentage of their money from a client. (More on this later).

I, on the other hand, am from a niche IFM service provider. One of my major goals is to promote enhanced staff competencies and long-term retention for the good of the integrated whole.

Therefore, when I begin working with the team at all levels I need to reassure them on this point. My tone and tenor, which is genuine, is: "I'm here to help you, not to oust you." My goal is to share my playbook with them, elicit their feedback, help them grow their skills, and leave them with an array of tools from the toolbox and make the staff into master craftsman driving excellence in their department.

Conducting the Interview and Assessment

In terms of related departments/business units, the interview/assessment process starts with Finance, because before any of the other areas can function or be implemented they must have financial/budget approval from the Finance/Accounting Department. The process finishes with Information Technology, because that is the boat that ensures this marriage among all of the business units stays afloat.

The following are some of the key indicators I am looking for in my assessment of these departments and some of the questions that naturally arise in each.

Finance: I first will examine how the organization manages its budget, accounts payable, general ledger, and chart of accounts related to IFM. How do they determine capital and operation budgets associated with commissioning new real estate properties added to their company's portfolio? What are the strategies employed for justifying and managing capital and operations budget increases? How do they balance budget reductions and increases in IFM?

Real Estate: Is the real estate portfolio effectively managed? How is the use of space managed in and outside of buildings? Is there a defined policy and procedure for managing lease contract owner and tenant obligations? Is the internal leadership across the IFM departments aware of areas of obligations? Does Real Estate use its own technology? Do IFM departments understand commissioning (standing up a new real estate property) versus decommissioning (closing a property) ownership levels, also known as (RACI)?

- R = Responsible
- A = Accountable
- C = Consulted
- I = Informed

Construction: What is the capital budget and project timeline? Are their key building specification standards, "source-to-spec"? Who are my key stakeholders internal and externally? Is the construction team working hand-in-hand with real estate, facilities, and supply chain? How is quality control and safety measured? What is the process for vendor selection? Is Supply Chain the owner of third-party vendor contracting? Is sustainability critical? Does construction use their own technology?

Facilities: First I look at the foundational considerations that drive Facilities. Does the organization have a formal IFM Strategy? Is Facilities aligned with Construction on vendor selection and awards or handed over construction predefined vendors? Is Facilities clear on real estate property ownership obligations? Is Facilities over vendor selection and management or is the senior leadership across the organization? Does Facilities manage their own vendor contract management and performance? Are multiple vendors used to perform "like" services or standardized and rationalized? Are vendors measured contractually based on defined scope of work, pricing, performance service level agreement, and key performance indicators? Does Facilities utilize its own technology?

Next, I assess how they optimize costs. Are the IFM division's chart of accounts structured in alignment with industry standards? Does a policy and procedure manual exist for distinguishing capital versus operational costs? If so, is it widely recognized and utilized by leadership? Additionally, is there a clearly defined process for checks and balances to ensure third-party vendor expenses are accurately categorized as capital or operational costs by IFM management?

Supply Chain: Does supply chain own all organization vendor contracting processes? Is there a defined vendor management program all vendors must adhere to, prior to successfully obtaining a company contract to deliver products and services? Is there a company vendor master service agreement all vendors must use or are contracts on vendor legal contract paper? Does the master service agreement include all key industry standard exhibits, real estate property listing, insurance, etc. requirements to mitigate company risk? Is Supply Chain managing costs or costs managed a departmental unit levels? Does Supply Chain use their own technology?

Are their vendor contracts, also known as "master service agreements," written on vendor or company contract paper, standardized, and do they contain clearly defined and delineated scopes of work, inclusive of all proper exhibits? Are departments using many third-party service providers providing same services or rationalized to a few? Are the departments following best practices for realizing and sustaining measurable cost savings? How well are they managing the financial impact of third-party services when they need to be increased or expanded?

Information Technology (IT): IT is instrumental in managing company cybersecurity and technology associated risk used throughout the company. Is IT and InfoSecurity reviewing each business units technology or is each department able to contract with any third-party software-as-a-service or cloud-based external company? Are there duplicate or similar technologies used among business units or is there an internal collaboration to ensure seamless data flow, data quality, end user training, vendor program management, etc.?

My interview/assessment process to get a comprehensive picture of this organization's present-day identity status naturally ends with information technology, because my process is essentially a diagnostic data-collection effort. I don't like to call it that, but that's what it is. As I go through my process, early on I often start getting inklings that some things are amiss.

For example, during my assessment, Finance needs to demonstrate an ability to quickly provide me with high-quality information I need for comprehensive analysis. They also need to be able to present the data and documented policies and procedures for how they manage costs (capital versus operational expenses) and those used by departments to track budget-to-actuals a part of IFM budgets. If they can't provide that in a timely fashion (or at all) then there it is likely that financial acumen impacts the ability of all business units to correctly and effectively track and allocate costs. It doesn't matter to me what their reports illustrate, or their management asserts, achieving realized measurable savings is never going to truly happen until Finance and Accounts Payable can encapsulate, document, train, and audit enterprise financials in a uniformed and structured manner.

Nothing happens in IFM without a steady, reliable stream of physical data that people can get their hands on when they need it. I have provided an overview in this chapter of the data you need for this assessment, but I will break it down in detail in coming chapters, and bring it all together in Chapter 8. Only when you get that core information at your fingertips can you forecast, and know where you are at all times. And that goes for all of the IFM-related business units and their core considerations.

This is where technology comes in to keep the marriage afloat—with transparency. Just like in a real marriage, you have nothing without it. Most people in facilities-related entities never have true transparency with regard to their costs. The executive does, so a few key indicators of the effectiveness of leaders is how well they optimize and rationalize vendors, and how well they communicate with their people about how that process is done throughout the business units. Defined processes require strong business unit leaders who lead by example and as a coach to their staff "players."

If you trust your data and your platform is intuitive, one thing technology does well is allow you to look in the mirror. It also allows leaders to provide transparency and give their team members the power at their fingertips to effectively monitor and manage the department's core considerations and collaborate with others. So as you explore the following chapters and the core considerations for all of the business units, keep the data in mind.

In this book, starting with Chapter 3, I will detail all of the departments/business units mentioned above. But first in Chapter 2 I want to examine particular aspects of three of those areas together as an example to set the stage for where the challenges of unity originate and how they can be overcome.

Chapter 2

The Engagement of Facilities and Supply Chain

Connect the dots between individual roles and the goals of the organization. When people see that connection, they get a lot of energy out of work.

–Ken and Scott Blanchard

When I go into an organization and start my interview and assessment process, my first considerations are foundational. Through examining finance first and then the other departments/business units, I start getting toward the bedrock answers in where the organization sits with respect to integrated facilities management (IFM) unity.

I know right away there is a unity problem when the people in Finance and Accounts Payable have trouble quickly producing two things:

DOI: 10.4324/9781003773955-3

1. Current, intensive analytics from high-quality data about how the organization manages facilities-related costs and measures realized cost savings.
2. Written policies and procedures used in the other departments to help manage those costs.

This usually means that the uniformity and structure needed for true IFM-system success is lacking. The best place to look for these deficits is in the relationship between two units—Supply Chain and Facilities. Let's start at what I call the core: Supply Chain.

Understanding the Connection Between Supply Chain Operations and IFM

In IFM as I envision it, the supply chain department/business unit should do what it does best—guaranteeing the smooth and efficient flow of necessary materials, equipment, and services required for facility maintenance, operations, and repairs. To effectively optimize facility performance and control costs, Supply Chain essentially acts as the central hub for coordinating procurement, inventory, delivery logistics, and vendor relationships.

That last thing—coordinating vendor relationships—is the key to accomplishing everything listed before that. IFM requires a solid vendor management program, and that is where supply chain should lead. In a perfect world, if you're running a vendor management program, it should always start with supply chain defining the rules of engagement with vendors for the entire IFM system.

In many organizations this doesn't happen. More often than not, I see Supply Chain running independently of

Facilities—not having a part in any contracting discussions. That approach is flawed.

When I look at Supply Chain's role in IFM, I see the word *integrated* as meaning that supply chain is not just a hub, but instead like the core atom of a molecule. They either take on 100% of contracting responsibility, from the request for proposal to writing the agreement, or they become a complement to facilities and coach them through the process, and then facilities manages the agreements.

What I see happening out there in the real world are three things, either A, B, or C:

A. Supply Chain has no part of contracting, meaning facilities is on its own.
B. Supply Chain has been directed to be a complement to the process, not owning the physical contract, but still a part of it, and they still let Facilities run the contract.
C. Supply Chain is in charge of all contracting, and that has come about as part of an organizational change directed by either a COO or an outside facilities management provider that has been brought on board.

You might look at Supply Chain's list of responsibilities in the first paragraph of this section and ask, "But doesn't supply chain have enough on its plate without owning all of the vendor management?" My response is that in IFM, if they don't own vendor management, they can forget about "guaranteeing" anything else on their extensive to-do list.

If a client is proficient, supply chain owns the process and it's their job then to educate their other business line leaders on vendor management, including construction and facilities, so they can pick that up and manage it. But that rarely happens.

Creating Clarity Around Ownership Rather Than Division

Having top management draw a line in the sand around Supply Chain's ownership of the master service agreement (MSA) is an example of creating role clarity in IFM and setting up business rules around it. Keep in mind this is very different from setting up turf or creating silos. By having separate facilities and Supply Chain business units the goal is not to create a separation between what the goals of the IFM strategy are and how each unit gets there. We are talking about a separation of competencies.

Do you believe that the average member of your Supply Chain team has the depth of knowledge and industry experience to know everything it takes to create a facilities-related contract? Do they know who the high-quality service providers in the industry are in 20 or 30 different facilities-related categories or what is involved with the scope of work of a fire, life, and safety vendor? Do they understand how determine the necessary specs for a chiller in a given facility?

Do They Even Know What a Chiller Is?

The answers to these questions is no. Supply Chain people for the most part are generalists at best when it comes to what is happening in Facilities, but what they do know how to do is create the core elements of a solid contract. Competent Supply Chain people also know how to standardize, consolidate, and rationalize vendors of products and services, which is something people in facilities can be downright terrible at. And Supply Chain people are experts on how to get a product or service to a certain place so it will be there at the time it is needed.

Competent Facilities people know how to turn a wrench (which goes much deeper than physically doing that; I'll explain later) along with knowing how to operate facilities. They also have the best handle on what they are looking for in different categories of facilities-related vendors. They are not typically adept at writing good contracts, in my experience.

On the other hand, most people in Supply Chain don't know much about the complex world of managing facilities, and until they're contributing expertise and sharing it, they don't have great answers themselves, because the Supply Chain people can't speak the world of facilities management. But when Facilities and Supply Chain do combine effectively, you get strong contracts. You get centralized contract management, and you get reduced risk because you have defined scopes of work about what a third-party person coming into your buildings should be doing at a specific rate.

If I'm a Facilities manager and I hire an HVAC company to come in and manage my boilers, chillers and cooling towers, what I call a good contract might have 50 pages. Most people freak out at 50-page contract. To me that substantial detail means I've done a much better job, versus having five pages. The time put in on the front end of a contract always pays off for everyone in the IFM system.

Focusing on the Master Service Agreement

In my assessment of an organization, one of my biggest clues about disunity is the lack of a MSA. I find this clue by asking someone in Supply Chain to show me one of their recent vendor contracts, and then I ask someone in Facilities to show me one of theirs. Most of the time they look completely different.

Without this most fundamental, simple template within the organization there cannot be true unity around facilities management. From a developmental point of view, an institutionalized MSA is what I would call "infancy" in integration, and then from there other layers build until there is a mature structure for managing vendors and their costs.

An MSA answers 70% of what you would normally need in any contract. Our primary focus with having a standardized structure is not to make things easy for everyone, though making things less complicated is a good thing, and it does that. The primary goal is standardization that seeks to reduce the risk that an organization might inherit form a contract, because it's that organization's contract, on their paper, with their terms and conditions. With an MSA undergirding a contract, you take away the vendor's ability to craft overly favorable language for themselves.

The other 30% of the contract consists of the exhibits—also called collectively the service line agreement (SLA)—which includes pricing, the scope of work, necessary insurance, licenses, and indemnification clauses. That 30% is going to be different in Supply Chain contracts versus facilities contracts versus construction contracts, etc., but the 70% meat of the contract is going to be identical for all of them.

Your core language of a contract should be synonymous. The only thing that should be different is in regard to a specific service that is being rendered. Every contract I pick up should look identical except for that 30%. And it does save time value and money in the long run. Think of just what this saves in your organization in legal fees: When attorneys review your contracts, they will know that unless it's a redline, 70% of each contract should look identical, so they don't have to bother with that part.

At one of the top three leading group purchasing organizations where I worked years ago we had something we called the stoplight: red, yellow, and green. It was brilliant. The red light represented the core areas of a contract you cannot change. What you can change is green. What might straddle the line is yellow (indemnification is one area off the top of my head where the border might be murky and might need clarification). This simplified red light example can be used unilaterally in an organization. *Don't touch it, this section is red.* If the vendor wants to try and strike that language, we tell them we have to get our attorney.

When we are talking about streamlining procurement processes, which I will detail in Chapter 5 on Supply Chain, that vendor MSA comes in very handy. It works equally well for the Facilities department in streamlining facilities operations and management. All of your contractors are going to be different, but you're still using the master to the degree you can.

So, whether we are addressing facilities, or construction, or whatever, C-suite management emphasizes throughout the IFM enterprise that Supply Chain owns the vendor MSA. Supply Chain essentially gives Facilities the MSA and says:

> This is 70% of the template for your vendor service agreements, and you and your vendors can't touch it. You just add to this the part you are expert in.

Facilities owns that 30% part of the contract, but supply chain still has a stake in it. Does that make things clear? If Facilities is to own its SLA, what does ownership mean? Does it mean that Supply Chain has nothing to do with the Facilities part of the contract? Does it mean that Facilities is to manage the contracts that are written and owned by supply chain? That's where you're setting up the separation of competencies and the rules of engagement.

Role Clarity and Accountability: The Framework for Unity

Back to the issue of silos versus separation of competencies. The difference here is I'm talking about who is best at certain things and where you put them in an IFM system based on those skillsets, not where the K-rails are between departments. I'm talking about creating role clarity and accountability. This is the foundation of the Responsible, Accountable, Consulted, and Informed (RACI) framework, which was developed in the 1950s and is most often credited to management structure and organization systems authority Edmond F. Sheehan. It is still in wide use today.

Figure 2.1 represents how the RACI matrix ties together the personnel and operations of Supply Chain and Facilities in a true IFM system.

The Role Clarity and Accountability (RACI) framework defines clear roles and responsibilities across all teams, optimizing both internal and external engagements to ensure alignment and efficiency. The framework is as follows:

R – Responsible: The individuals or teams tasked with execution, ensuring accountability at the operational level. Basically, these are the people who are actively engaged in completing the task.

A – Accountable: The person who owns the task, ensures its completion, and makes final decisions. There should be only one accountable individual per task.

C – Consulted: Key stakeholders who must be involved in decision making or that provide necessary expertise and advice during task execution.

I – Informed: Individuals not directly involved in decision making but who need who need to be kept updated on task progress to ensure transparency and communication.

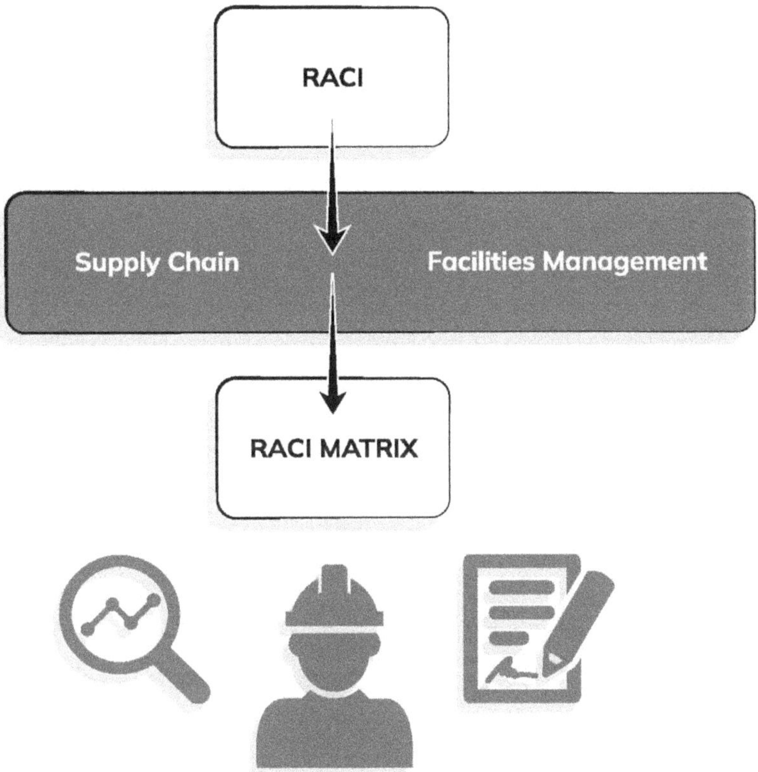

Figure 2.1 Tying supply chain and facilities together through the Role Clarity and Accountability (RACI) framework. (Figure content and concept created by the author.)

The purpose of this framework is to prevent confusion and overlapping responsibilities by clearly outlining *who* is responsible for the *what* on a project.

Let's use fire, life, and safety vendors as an example. One of my healthcare clients had 285 clinics in seven states. Facilities had approximately 80 different fire, life, and safety service providers. That's not optimization—it's saturation. So could Supply Chain assist with this challenge without expertise in Facilities? Sure they could. They certainly have

Table 2.1 Sample IFM RACI Matrix Page

Deliverable	*Finance*	*Real Estate*	*Construction*	*Facilities*	*Supply Chain*	*IT*
Capital Budget Approval	A	C	C	C	C	C
Site Selection & Lease Execution	C	A/R	I	C	C	I
Construction Planning & Permits	I	C	A/R	C	I	C
Store/Site Build-Out	I	C	A/R	C	I	C
Facilities Equipment Installation	C	I	C	A/R	I	I
IT Infrastructure Setup	C	I	C	C	I	A/R
Vendor Sourcing & Procurement	C	I	C	C	A/R	C
Asset Tagging & Inventory	I	I	C	C	A/R	C
Operational Readiness/Go-Live	C	C	C	A/R	C	C
Ongoing Maintenance/Facilities Mgmt	I	I	I	A/R	C	C
Cost Tracking & Variance Reporting	A/R	I	C	C	C	I

extensive experience in creating and overseeing a bidding process that could effectively whittle down this list.

But how do you create a bid if you don't know the particulars that go into it? If you don't know the industry, you'll be eaten like chum in the water. That is where the RACI framework comes in.

First, you identify all the tasks in the project, list all the key decisions that will have to be made around them. That's the *what*. Then you assign clear roles for each of the tasks, designating *who* is Responsible, Accountable, Consulted, and Informed. I do this using a RACI matrix (or chart) that defines and clarifies roles and responsibilities of all of the stakeholders. Table 2.1 shows an example page from a RACI matrix.

Defining roles in this way improves communication and collaboration, because every team member understands their roles and responsibilities. When accountability is assigned for owning tasks, people don't have to question who they should go to when they need updates or have issues with a process in question. When everyone know who is responsible for, say, furniture and millwork versus medical and information technology projects at a given stage, confusion is reduced, and considerable time is spared.

Conclusion

In IFM system Utopia, supply chain and facilities work together seamlessly. They coordinate how goods and services within flow within and among buildings and complexes. Together they collaborate on optimizing space, meeting maintenance needs, and managing inventory. They share data that is integrated with each other and with that of finance/ accounting, so when demand in goods and services fluctuates they are ready to adjust in real time to ensure efficient operations across the entire IFM enterprise.

When I am conducting my initial appraisal of departmental alignment in IFM, the aforementioned high level of role clarity and accountability (or lack thereof) combined with data integration (or lack thereof) shows up early in my process. As I mentioned at the beginning of this chapter, I start in Finance, and what I am evaluating there first is the methodology the IFM enterprise uses to define realized cost savings, and then the methods they use to track and improve on them.

Chapter 3

Finance: Our Partner in Getting to Realized Cost Savings

Beware of little expenses; a small leak will sink a great ship.
–Benjamin Franklin

The Need to Demonstrate Realized Savings Through Integrated Facilities Management (IFM)

The ecosystem of healthcare, in which my facilities expertise developed and matured, has never been an easy place to operate, not only from the perspective of its inherent "extra layer of burden" that I laid out in the Introduction, but also its financial realities. They can be bleak at times.

DOI: 10.4324/9781003773955-4

The recent past is no exception. In February 2025, Kaufman Hall released its "National Hospital Flash Report" on CY 2024, which showed that 37% of hospitals in the country were losing money despite intensive initiatives designed to recover from the pandemic. But look at the bright side: that's down a whole three percentage points from 2023 when 40% of hospitals were underwater. This slow progress came despite the booming economy and an increase of operating revenue of 9% per calendar day over the previous year. Overall expenses per calendar day rose 6% over 2023, but supply and drug expenses shot up 9% each.

The following are the major areas leadership of hospitals and health systems are focusing on to become more productive and create cost savings, according to Kaufman Hall representatives:

- Reducing contract labor by developing the internal talent pipeline.
- Using digital technology and AI to support the workforce and streamline operations. (Dyrda, 2025)

These two bullets are highly relevant to how we need to focus our attention on cost saving in IFM.

A Necessary Start in Realized Savings: Analyzing and Cleansing Data

Efforts to achieve realized savings, as they are often carried out, are akin to initiating an after-action report: "Let's see what happened, and if we didn't achieve realized cost savings this time let's see what we did wrong and what we can do to fix it."

Realizing cost savings cannot be a retrospective exercise. It must happen in real time, in the moment. But first we need to have a baseline, so we can take an initial look backward that we can rely on. Achieving realized savings through IFM goes far beyond gathering financial numbers with your fingers crossed behind your back. In addition to interdepartmental collaboration, it takes clean, "normalized" data and robust analytics capabilities.

In my assessment of an IFM enterprise I begin by reviewing and cleaning financial data from the past 24 months related to accounts payable and purchase card transactions to ensure accuracy and integrity. This process includes identifying any inconsistencies, discrepancies, duplicate payments, and fraudulent activities. It also entails correcting errors, ensuring compliance with financial policies, and preparing for strategic financial decision making.

Beyond preparing a dataset to ensure its accuracy, reliability, and consistency for financial analysis and reporting, this cleansing process serves several valuable functions, including:

- Enhancing the ability to generate reliable audit, budgeting, and forecasting reports.
- Improving cash flow by correcting erroneous payments.
- Aiding in detecting and preventing fraud through pattern recognition.
- Helping to identify spending anomalies or inefficiencies for process improvement.
- Ensuring data accuracy for financial statements and tax reporting.
- Facilitating benchmarking against past performance and industry standards.
- Supporting strategic decision making by providing a clean, reliable dataset for analysis.

Cases in Achieving Realized IFM Savings

The following are two examples in my experience that demonstrate what is involved. They show why I chose to first emphasize in the previous chapter the connection of Supply Chain and Facilities, and two of the major elements that drive that connection—the vendor master agreements and service line agreements. These agreements are comprehensive contracts defining the business terms between a company and its suppliers for purchasing goods or services, hammered out in advance.

Case #1: In March 2024, I was hired by the second-largest children's clinic network in the United States to temporary take over leadership of its IFM enterprise, which meant overseeing $60 million in financials across their 279 clinics spread among seven different states. Through my initial assessment, I was able to identify and get to work on several financial, operational, and technological opportunities, including financial reengineering, staff development, and implementing new programs and emerging technologies. new program and technology implementation. It is important to note that in aligning the enterprise for cost savings you can create wide-ranging positive effects in the organization far beyond the business units involved in the IFM enterprise. In this case, we were able to drive collaboration and strategic alignment across multiple vital departments, including Accounting, Finance, Infectious Disease and Quality Management, Information Technology, Legal, and Risk Management.

A significant financial optimization achievement in this process was the reduction of annual expenditure from $60M to $11M. This dramatic improvement stemmed primarily from two strategic actions:

1. Correction of Financial Misclassification
Initially, the Capital Expenses (CapEx) were incorrectly categorized under the Operational Expenses (OpEx) budget, an oversight by the Finance department known as *budget misclassification*. By diligently realigning these expenditures to their correct accounting categories, a substantial portion of the previously inflated expenses due to this error—was accurately repositioned, significantly decreasing the OpEx spend.

2. Vendor Rationalization and Optimization Savings
By strategically analyzing and rationalizing vendor relationships, we delivered an additional **$1.3 million in cost savings**. Through careful vendor optimization, consolidating services, renegotiating agreements, and eliminating redundancies, we streamlined procurement processes, enhancing overall budget efficiency.

Collectively, these corrective and proactive measures not only rectified previous accounting inaccuracies but also established sustainable financial practices, resulting in considerable ongoing savings.

Other important achievements in this process included:

- Developing a new enterprise financial model, which enabled the organization to identify and prioritize essential clinics for investment based on various critical metrics such as capital, census, insurance, and operational allocation.
- Implementing an internal IFM program to ensure long-term sustainability, and launching new initiatives, including introducing computerized maintenance management system (CMMS), a vendor master program and establishing key performance indicators (KPIs) and service line agreements.

- Introducing technology that provided financial and operational transparency, combining capital and operational expenses, identifying opportunities for localized vendor contracting, and rationalizing the number of similar service providers.
- Leveraging new technologies that helped with real estate/lease administration, janitorial and security system management, and vendor contract management.

Case #2: In a different project in spring of 2022 I was brought on to another organization to review $38 million in capital equipment and variable construction project work across a client's 246 U.S. medical offices. I was given three dozen data files along with supporting project information to normalize and then analyze. I consolidated these files and moved them into an online data visualization tool, enabling me to show where each HVAC asset was located in each of the real estate properties real estate. I then created Requests for Proposal (RFPs) concurrently with new standardized master service agreements for the organization in HVAC, Project Management and Roofing Project Management, HVAC, and Roofing. I also collaborated with the company's senior executive and accounting engineering teams to developed their 2023 capital master plan. As a result, SolvingX was able to provide cost transparency where it was previously was foggy. Assets in HVAC were missing and there were inaccuracies in tracking capital costs, age of equipment and other key data points. Today, the fog has been lifted, and the capital budget has been lowered by several millions, while missing equipment lifecycle asset data have been collected to identify future replacement needs.

All of the elements addressed above form an overview of the many facets involved in achieving realized savings, and they will continue to run as a thread throughout much of this book. In Chapters 4 and 5 on Facilities and Supply Chain I will delve more into the service line agreements and their associated KPIs, along with the rationalization of service providers/suppliers that are presented in the cases above and why they are key to creating the tie-back to Finance in achieving realized savings. In Chapter 8 I will address the data quality and technology proficiencies that help to make that connection happen smoothly.

For now in this chapter we turn to budget management in IFM—specifically how to balance the inevitable and continual budget reductions and increases that are part of the business of facilities management.

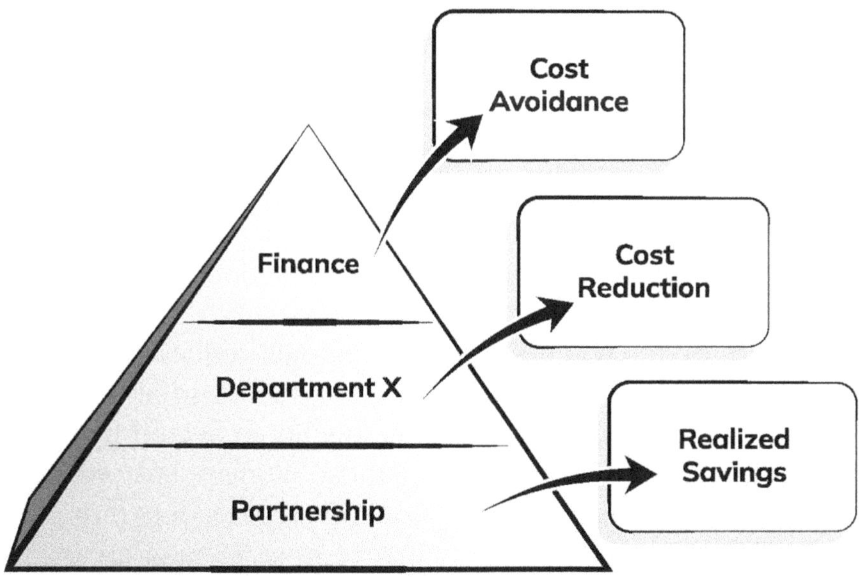

Figure 3.1 The Partnerships among IFM business units and finance, and their considerations. (Figure content and concept created by the author.)

As we turn to budget management, Figure 3.1 represents the overarching issues driving the relationships among each of the IFM business units and Finance.

Budget Management: Balancing Budget Reductions and Increases in IFM

In facilities management, budgets fluctuate considerably. This is due in large part to two processes that affect all of the IFM business units like few others:

- Commissioning, which happens when we open a new building or complex that we either built new or recently acquired.
- Decommissioning, which happens when we let go of an old building or complex.

These two issues will be covered in detail, particularly in the next chapter on the responsibilities of the Facilities business unit, but also in many areas of the book. For the purposes of Finance, though, it is important to recognize, which should be obvious, that these two actions can cause large swings and reallocations in budgets.

What happens when systemwide budget reductions must be made and IFM is expected to tighten their budgets while still maintaining the level of service quality expected by top leadership, and more importantly, those ultimate customers—patients and families. In these situations IFM leaders must work with top leadership and Finance in four major areas:

- Navigating budget reductions while maintaining service quality.

- Implementing strategies for justifying and managing capital and operations budget increases.
- Balancing budget expansion with the use of third-party services.
- Managing the financial impact of third-party vendor expansion.

These budget management priorities and solutions are detailed below:

Navigating Budget Reductions While Maintaining Service Quality

- *Prioritize Core Services*: Identify mission-critical operations using a tiered service model. Focus limited resources on functions that directly affect safety, compliance, and business continuity.
- *Implement Preventive Maintenance:* Shift from reactive to proactive maintenance to reduce emergency repair costs and extend asset life without increasing spend.
- *Leverage Data and KPIs*: Use building performance metrics to identify inefficiencies and justify strategic reallocations. Transparency builds trust with stakeholders when implementing cuts.
- *Optimize Staffing Models*: Cross-train employees and adjust shifts or roles to reduce overtime and maximize workforce utility without reducing headcount.
- *Engage in Vendor Collaboration*: Work with service providers to renegotiate terms, bundle contracts, or adopt shared-risk models that maintain output while easing cost pressures.

Implementing Strategies for Justifying and Managing Capital and Operations Budget Increases

- *Build a Data-Driven Case*: Use historical cost data, condition assessments, and life-cycle projections to justify budget requests. Demonstrate return on investment (ROI) and risk avoidance.
- *Align with Strategic Goals*: Show how budget increases support environmental, social, and governance goals, resilience planning, or regulatory compliance. Frame facilities as enablers, not just cost centers.
- *Communicate in Executive Language*: Convert technical needs into business impacts—think downtime, liability, brand perception, or employee productivity.
- *Phase Large Investments*: Break capital projects into phases to spread financial load while still moving forward. Pilot programs can reduce perceived risk.
- *Document and Forecast Clearly*: Provide transparent reporting, scenario modeling, and five-year outlooks to build leadership confidence in your stewardship.

Balancing Budget Expansion with the Use of Third-Party Services

- *Assess Make-or-Buy Rationally*: Use a total cost of ownership analysis to decide between in-house expansion and outsourcing. Include quality, control, and speed-to-deploy factors.
- *Conduct Strategic Outsourcing, Not Cost Dumping*: Choose third parties that offer value beyond cost—like innovation, technology access, or industry certifications.
- *Maintain Oversight and Governance*: Budget expansions often bring complexity. Embed performance clauses,

service level agreements (SLAs), and audit mechanisms to ensure third-party accountability.

- *Communicate Internal Value Protection*: Reassure staff and unions (if applicable) that budget increases support internal teams via upskilling or oversight roles.
- *Blend Flexibility into Contracts*: Allow scope shifts in vendor agreements to scale services up or down with facility needs—maximizing financial responsiveness.

Managing the Financial Impact of Third-Party Vendor Expansion

- *Track Cost-to-Value Metrics*: Don't just monitor spend—track productivity, downtime, or quality benchmarks to measure vendor ROI and justify continued outsourcing.
- *Build an Integrated Financial View*: Combine internal and vendor budgets to see holistic impacts. This prevents silos and enables smarter portfolio-level decisions.
- *Use Performance-based Incentives*: Tie financial incentives to outcomes (not just deliverables), promoting efficiency and innovation from vendors.
- *Factor in Hidden Costs*: Consider onboarding, oversight, transition risks, and exit clauses when projecting vendor-related budgets. Don't understate long-term obligations.
- *Regularly Benchmark Vendors*: Compare your partners against industry peers to ensure you're paying competitive rates for competitive performance.

IFM Asset Management and Capital Planning and Their Effects on Finance

In the next chapter on Facilities I will detail responsibility for asset management, and in Chapter 6, (the Real Estate/ Construction chapter) I will explore capital planning more extensively, but for now I want to explain how these closely related responsibilities affect financial accounting in the IFM enterprise.

Simply put, a capital asset can be anything that is durable and has significant value. It can be anything from a building to a painting, or from a piece of furniture to a chiller. Capital assets represent any expense you can depreciate for tax purposes. That is, if you recognize it for its value and ability to be depreciated. This is another thing that often does not happen, in my experience. For example, in helping an organization move from Chicago to Charlotte, I noticed they had quite a bit of fancy, commissioned art pieces on the walls. So as we were building out and preparing to move, I asked to see what they had for art pieces in their asset database. You can guess what I'm going to tell you next, right?

That's right—they had nothing. Someone could have stolen a piece of art, and then good luck ever tracking it down, because it was never recorded as an asset.

This reporting and recording is typically the responsibility of Facilities, and I will cover that later, but just as in our CMMS example earlier in this chapter, it hits home in Finance, when suddenly a considerable bit of value is missing, but the IFM enterprise can't tell you where and when it went missing.

Poorly written capital plans can be expensive to an organization. Doing this type of planning successfully starts with a reasonable definition of what qualifies as a capitalized expense. You can't set up something arbitrary like a value $500, because nowadays a good office chair that doesn't destroy your back will run at least that much. So every chair in the building can't be a capitalized expense. That is why Finance should own the process for determining what is and what is not a capital expense.

The next thing to keep in mind is that just because something is not a capitalized, depreciated asset, it is still an asset, and therefore needs to be tracked and treated as such. Here is a question that explains why that is: "Why are our Steelcase ergonomic brand office chairs only lasting half as long as our Herman Miller ergonomic brand chairs, even though they both cost $600?" That's an asset-related, data-driven piece of information you need to know if you are going to realize cost savings. In fire, life, and safety, as another example, you need to track every sprinkler head and every control panel, just as you track every chiller. Those first two aren't capitalized expenses like the chiller, but having all of those items as assets in your work order management system is vital because otherwise you can't track the repairs or predict the end of life. And Finance needs to know you are doing that.

Right-Sizing the General Ledger for IFM

Getting the general ledger right-sized is critical in IFM for aligning the financial strategy with operational goals and creating financial transparency in facilities management as a whole. In this section I want to address strategies for right-sizing the general ledger to meet organizational needs, while balancing governance and accountability to deliver sustained cost reductions amid cost-of-living pressures.

In the interest of alignment and transparency in IFM, I see Finance's major responsibility as ensuring everything is set up correctly for reporting and analysis. This just doesn't happen as much as I would like to see, and that is due to many reasons. Often financial people don't understand the world of facilities, but they do should know how to collaborate and set that structure up and follow industry guidelines. Examples of financial guidelines for facilities measurement are BOMA (https://boma.org/boma-standards/). For capital planning/

operational budgeting, the CSI Master Format for Construction (www.csiresources.org/standards/overview) should be followed.

Often Facilities people don't understand the language of Finance. O.K., that's normal, but not speaking the same language throughout the organization on the chart of accounts should never become normalized. That's inviting chaos. This should be intuitive when creating any business structure, but still it often doesn't happen.

For example, I had one client who had pest control combined with janitorial on the chart of accounts. Those are two completely different industries, and they should not be combined if you want the data in the general ledger to effectively and efficiently track costs and savings.

Then there are other instances in which I will find there are missing items/categories on the chart of accounts, and I mean vital items that cover some of IFM's biggest expenses. For example: How am I going to track down to the cost level if I am missing HVAC as a sub-category on the chart of accounts? Believe me, it happens. In a case like that, the Finance team has to do the best they can do with whatever piggy bank they're given and apply those associated costs to whatever is in that chart of account structure.

This is why the chart of accounts needs to be set up by Finance in collaboration with Facilities, because that chart of accounts forms the structure of the general ledger and is the key piece at the end of a long process. One example is when a process starts with your CMMS, or work order management system, or ticket system—whatever you call it. The more thorough you are in setting up your ledger, the better, for obvious reasons. The most crucial of those reasons is the pursuit of data quality, because we don't want to put garbage in and end up getting garbage out, which happens too much.

This may seem elementary to some, but I'm going to go through it anyway. The following is how things should happen in eight or ten easy steps in the CMMS scenario:

1. A ticket is generated for fixing changing an expansion valve on an air conditioning unit.
2. That ticket then creates a work order that is then sent to a vendor.
3. The vendor is then informed that they need to provide a service, which they intend to provide at the cost specified in the SLA in their contract.
4. The vendor then performs the work and sends you an invoice.
5. Facilities reviews the invoice and approves it.
6. At this point the process transitions from purchase order status to an invoice, which means it heads to Finance.
7. Finance either stamps the invoice or sends it back to Facilities with a dispute or a question.
8. Once the invoice is approved, the vendor gets paid, and the cost data goes into a bucket—i.e., whatever account assignment Finance thinks makes the most sense in the general ledger.

There are so many places this can go wrong, like in the third bullet, where we assume the vendor has a contract and a solid SLA written in collaboration between Facilities and Supply Chain. This is not a hiccup in the process; it is more like a ripple or a tidal wave when it comes to getting realized cost savings at the end, because without a formal contract, vendors are going to charge you whatever they say their rate is.

Also, in item 8, if the chart of accounts is either sorely lacking in detail or highly overwhelming in it, two separate processes whose steps 1 through 7 are absolutely identical can end up with their cost data going into two different buckets.

And so goes your ability to track whether you are actually realizing cost savings in a given account. That is why having a general ledger of optimal size is so critical, and why Finance needs to own that process, with help from Facilities. This is also true with all of the other business units in the IFM enterprise

Conclusion

In the age of AI, our data is often being collected in this moment, and the next. That can be a good thing, but we need to keep transparency in mind, up and down the line. Our systems need to be structured so people can handle them without misallocating expense, and CapEx and OpEx need to be separate. Leadership is not doing their job of managing the budget if there is not complete financial transparency. If they are putting their eyes to it and managing it, these anomalies begin to become fewer and fewer until they become obsolete—they never happen because they get corrected first far up the line.

References

Dyrda, L. (2025, February 27). 37% of hospitals still losing money. *Becker's Hospital Review*. www.beckershospitalreview.com/finance/37-of-hospitals-still-losing-money.html.

Kaufman Hall. (2025, February 4). National hospital flash report: December 2024 metrics. www.kaufmanhall.com/sites/default/files/2025-02/KH-NHFR_Report-December-2024-Metrics.pdf.

Chapter 4

Optimizing Facilities Management: A Strategic Approach

Strategy is not the consequence of planning, but the opposite: its starting point.

–Henry Mintzberg

Exploring the Roots of an Effective Integrated Facilities Management (IFM) Strategy

When I start digging in an organization, I am first trying to find whether there is a formal IFM strategy. More importantly, if there is one, I want to get a sense of whether anyone in any of the other business units outside of Facilities knows (or cares) about that strategy. There are often strong hints of that (either positive or negative) coming out of my queries in Finance/Accounting, but in Facilities I find out for sure.

DOI: 10.4324/9781003773955-5

You might think that if you were going to set out from scratch to build a truly IFM operation, you would just create a department/business unit called "Facilities Management" with its own Chief Executive Facilities Management Officer in the C-suite. Then you would pull parts of all of your current facilities-related entities underneath that umbrella and be done with it. Then you would never experience the problems of having all these different departments and the silos between them that create barriers to continuity. Right?

Wrong. I can almost guarantee you will eventually end up with the same challenges. The problem with that framework, going back to Responsible, Accountable, Consulted, and Informed (RACI), is that the professionals in each of those different areas have things that they do very well that the professionals in each of the others aren't so adept at.

Plus, those other entities have responsibilities and accountability in the organization that go beyond facilities-related considerations, as I noted with supply chain, so you would be unnecessarily draining their talent. I can't think of a more wasteful proposition than creating your own mini Supply Chain or Finance entities within a Facilities business unit. In essence, though, that is what happens when you don't have IFM—a massive duplication of effort.

In Chapter 2, I partly addressed vendor management (I've only begun to scratch the surface), where duplicated effort is evident in many organizations, but let's look at another good example.

Integrating the Real Estate Portfolio: Costs and Vendor Base

One IFM issue that has the greatest impact on marrying the Finance/Accounting, Real Estate, Construction, Facilities and

Supply Chain business units is commissioning (opening a new, or newly acquired, building or complex) and decommissioning (letting go of an old building or complex). I present commissioning/decommissioning as a single issue because I combine these terms in my mind.

Commissioning and decommissioning projects within an organization are inverse in nature, but in some ways they are one and the same. They both present an opportunity—either to manage an asset well or to create a money pit. How many organizations do it right? Very few in my experience.

Most people in the business units outside of Real Estate don't grasp the significance of these terms and the lessons they can take away from the process. Especially in Facilities and Supply Chain, people need to appreciate what it takes to close a building and terminate agreements with vendors and suppliers, just as much as they need to appreciate what it takes to add new services, implement standards, and supply flow when a building opens. Otherwise, unnecessary expenses accumulate and can continue to impact the bottom line

This is a great example of why cross-functional integration of departments is absolutely required in IFM, and why a formal IFM strategy and vendor management program are essential. Those suppliers and service vendors associated with that building you're either decommissioning or commissioning are not going to point out to you that they are still in there getting paid for a contract unless you terminate their agreement.

Should they alert you to that as a partner? Absolutely. Do they? In many cases, absolutely not. They're going to charge you to make their money, just like everybody else.

Here is where there is typically what I call a vertically integrated breakdown, because it is going to potentially involve the teams in Real Estate, Construction, Supply Chain, and Facilities, and then that all goes back up to the Chief Operating Officer (COO) and the Chief Financial Officer (CFO). Most of the time they, as leaders, put that onus on their department as they should, but they don't emphasize that working intertwined in this effort is a requirement.

You need that mandate from above, and you also need a cheat sheet. You need to be confident that when you commission or decommission you're locked and loaded, working in synergy and harmony to ensure your costs are managed for effectiveness, to increase our bottom line. This doesn't normally happen.

Whether you're commissioning or decommissioning, you have a rash of vendor contracting activity going on immediately. Use your house as an example, because it's essentially the same thing. For any house you buy, are you not going to need the same things? You're going to need utilities, you'll have to pay your mortgage to someone, you'll need landscaping if you have it, window cleaning if you don't do it yourself, HVAC repairs or replacement if the current system is inefficient or insufficient for your needs. And more.

So then back to our commercial real estate, where you have recurring maintenance agreements. You must decommission those. Terminating them and setting them up are equally important. That's where decommissioning/commissioning become almost synonymous, and it needs to be looked at with that mindset. There are some differences, but most organizations don't have that framework wired, because they're relying on different divisions operating in a state of disintegration. It's often just broken.

Having various facilities in scattered among different geographical regions compounds these problems. I recently completed a big project, consisting of 285 clinics in seven states, and that was classic example, not any different than what I've outlined above. They struggled, so it was my job to help bring that cheat sheet and synergy among their divisions.

It's a challenge. You want to believe that everyone's going to do the right thing and a lot of times it doesn't happen, and it should happen. But people are busy, and if you don't put in a considerable amount of work in the beginning to decrease the amount of work going forward, then you just continue what I call the cycle that broke. Nothing is going to change unless you invest that upfront extra time to decrease your overall time.

Streamlining Operations for Greater Efficiency

When executives ask me how I would go about streamlining their facilities operations they are often envisioning "smart" buildings that run themselves. While this kind of technology is evolving and I will have some good things to say about this later in the book when I talk about streamlining operations in Facilities, I primarily like to recommend hiring and retaining smart people.

A Turn of a Phrase Versus a Turn of the Wrench

In facilities management, there is a distinct difference between merely speaking about efficiency and truly achieving it—between "talking a good game" and actually "turning a wrench," as industry professionals often say. This distinction is particularly critical in healthcare facilities, where vital infrastructure depends heavily on skilled engineers and technicians. As the workforce responsible for running central plant operations (housing crucial mechanical, electrical, and plumbing systems) ages and approaches retirement, the pool of experienced IFM technicians shrinks dramatically. This looming shortage presents a genuine risk to the seamless operation of healthcare facilities, highlighting the urgent need for proactive workforce planning and skills development within the IFM industry.

This is troubling because many executives believe their only good option is to outsource facilities to a large IFM service provider. But I can tell you from having worked with the number one and two global-scale IFM providers, even those firms often rely on third-party service providers for repair and maintenance (R&M). Why? The engineers responsible for handling these work orders may not always have the ability to complete repairs internally. Several factors contribute to this reliance. Many companies prioritize hiring young, book-smart professionals who may lack hands-on experience.

Additionally, some engineering teams, depending on the facility's location or region, may not have access to engineers with the advanced qualifications—such as Master, Certified, or Specialized Certifications—required to handle more complex R&M tasks in mechanical, electrical, and plumbing systems. As a result, many engineers in these teams are still at the "Entry-Level" or "Journeyman" stage of their careers. These technicians can typically perform basic R&M tasks, but when it comes to managing aging equipment or assets, their lack of experience with older, complex systems can lead to outsourcing for more specialized tasks.

Furthermore, the overall employment cost of these newer hires—factoring in salary, benefits, and potential bonuses—is often lower compared to more experienced engineers who were not retained or transitioned during the shift to an IFM model.

Cost-cutting is another driving factor. In an effort to meet client savings expectations, many organizations reduce their full-time workforce, as labor costs are among the largest budget items. This shift leads to greater reliance on third-party vendors for essential R&M.

Another strategy often employed, though less discussed, is the "run-to-failure" approach. In this model, companies intentionally let equipment deteriorate until it fails, positioning the failure as a justification for replacement under capital expenses. While this tactic reduces ongoing R&M costs, it also generates additional revenue for the IFM provider, as new equipment and parts are often marked up. When combined with the fixed service fees in the master service agreement, this helps the provider meet cost-saving obligations, sometimes referred to as the "savings glide path."

In the world of facilities going forward, complementing proficiency at turning the wrench with the current and future technology is going to be highly valuable. As an organization you still need to have people who understand how to turn the wrench as well as being able to operationally manage the equipment along with whatever technology is helping them monitor and manage the equipment. Someone must have the mechanical engineering understanding of that equipment, especially where old infrastructure is the rule rather than the exception.

Having that historical legacy—for example, understanding where the mechanical, electrical and plumbing, or oil and gas runs throughout a complex hospital—is essential to efficient operations. You have to know it from the root cause to up-fitting, and to day-to-day managing because something is always going to happen.

Understanding the "Gearing Ratio"

Streamlining operation starts with the important key performance indicator (KPI) of self-performance, which is distinct from a mere metric or data point. It reflects an organization's commitment to maximizing in-house capabilities rather than outsourcing. For companies with in-house engineers, a key measure of self-performance is the percentage of work orders handled internally versus those contracted out. This directly impacts operational efficiency and cost-effectiveness. This is critical to streamlining operations because if full-time employees perform maintenance tasks, costs should be lower than hiring third-party vendors—particularly for engineering work. The key is ensuring that in-house teams are effectively utilized.

I refer to this as the "gearing ratio," adapted from its traditional financial meaning. In this context, it represents the proportion of wrench-turning performed by internal staff versus external contractors. A higher self-performance ratio generally means better cost control, provided in-house engineers have the necessary expertise.

Simply having full-time employees on payroll is not enough. Self-performance can be a money-saver, but only if your Full-time employees (FTEs) are proficient in personally handling a good number of your work orders. If an organization continues to rely heavily on outside HVAC vendors and other third parties, the intended cost savings and efficiency benefits of self-performance are lost.

Leveraging CMMS for Self-Performance Tracking

A well-structured computerized maintenance management system (CMMS) is essential for tracking effective self-performance. Every work order in a CMMS should capture key details by property location:

1. Work Order Information:
   - Date/Time opened and closed.
   - Assigned technician (in-house or third-party).
   - Hourly rate of service provider.
   - Check-in/Check-out times.
2. Asset Information:
   - Asset serial number.
   - Manufacturer and model details.
   - Supporting documentation (manuals, warranties).
3. R&M Details:
   - Classification (e.g., MEP).
   - Specific notes on the work completed.

Accurate CMMS data enables better decision-making regarding repairs, maintenance strategies, and performance tracking. While often referred to as a work order management system, it should function as much more—serving as a data-driven tool for asset management and KPI analysis.

Diagnosing Self-Performance Gaps

A CMMS also highlights gaps in self-performance. If internal teams handle only 40% of work orders while 60% are outsourced, the organization is falling short of a typical 70% self-performance target. The reasons could include:

- Lack of in-house expertise compared to external vendors.
- Insufficient staffing levels.

- Underperformance by in-house staff (a rare but possible issue).
- Aging equipment requiring more specialized repairs.

If outdated equipment is driving outsourcing, it may signal a need to reassess broader asset management KPIs rather than just self-performance. Identifying these root causes allows organizations to take corrective action, optimizing both costs and operational efficiency.

Again, the work order management system for needs to be much more than its name implies, and you will understand why when we get deeper into asset management and KPIs later in this chapter.

Having made the point about their value in asset management and having them do perhaps 70% of your work order tasks, from a management standpoint, having seasoned facilities engineers is helpful beyond turning wrenches. For that other 30% of the time they can play a vital role in managing your vendor base, versus a novice or a supply chain person.

When you put an inexperienced new hire or someone from procurement in front of an experienced HVAC vendor for facilities contract negotiations, it's like putting chum in the water.

They can sniff out within a few minutes of conversation whether your novice employee knows what a filter is versus a chiller versus a rooftop unit. Then they're going to ditch their Proposal B and sell them their preferred Proposal A, which is a bag full of fictitious needs. Conversely, if you put a seasoned engineer in front of that prospective vendor, their knowledge/experience base allows them to sniff out BS (bad stuff) from that vendor in mere seconds, and the vendor dispenses with the BS and out comes Proposal B.

Even with engineering, though, there are all levels of experts. So you are searching for that happy-medium expert within the community who can be trusted to help you write best-in-class service line agreement exhibits for your vendor contracts. Again, remember that in our contracts, Supply Chain is responsible for the master service agreement (70% of the contract) and Facilities is responsible for the service line agreement (the other 30%). We don't throw the procurement folks in the water with the sharks during negotiations, but we do let them do what they do best, which is create great contracts. That means we keep them Consulted and Informed on the RACI chart (as I presented in Chapter 2) in our vendor management program.

KPIs and Metrics in Facilities: More Than Just Managing Assets

The first account that comes to mind when people think of general ledgers is assets. In Facilities, we are all about assets and how they are managed. Our physical assets include not only the equipment, machinery and furnishings that most people in other professions concern themselves with, but also the very buildings and complexes in which those other basic assets reside.

In Chapter 3, I presented asset management from the view of what Finance and Accounting needs from the other IFM-related departments/business units. Although that view of asset management is aligned and coordinated with finance throughout the enterprise in true IFM, it turns into much more of a hands-on, boots-on affair when we get into Facilities.

Asset management involves tracking and managing assets, such as machinery, vehicles, or Information Technology (IT) equipment. This process goes through the useful life of an asset, from purchase to disposal. It includes monitoring asset condition, usage, maintenance schedules, and depreciation to optimize performance and lifespan (aka "asset lifecycle"). Effective asset management helps reduce unnecessary expenditures, improve maintenance strategies, and ensure compliance with safety standards.

In a peak-performing IFM system, we use asset registers to document all pertinent details about each asset. We implement intensive preventive maintenance programs to extend asset life and reduce operational disruptions. We continually monitor performance of our assets against benchmarks for efficiency, which coincides with Finance's asset depreciation schedule and cost-effectiveness. We manage the disposal or repurposing of assets in line with environmental regulations. We incorporate specialized technology such as radio frequency identification or internet of things smart objects for real-time asset tracking and management.

All of this supports our strategy, giving us insights into how we use assets and where we need to invest further. Risk management is integral to all of this, as I will detail later.

While asset management is a critical focus of our KPIs and metrics in Facilities, our extra layer of management focuses on the overall environment. As facilities managers we wholly own the maintenance and repair related to facility mechanical, electrical, plumbing (MEP), furniture, fixtures & equipment, and energy and utility costs. Note: fluctuating utility (electric and natural gas) costs can be a sign of a failing mechanical asset (e.g., chiller, boiler, cooling tower, etc.).

In addition to striving to extend the life of assets and maximize their value, we must also ensure that our facilities operate efficiently while effectively meeting the needs of the people who occupy, use, or otherwise come into contact with them. Through effective asset management we are helping to create those operational efficiencies, safe working environment, and meet the needs of our users. We do this through measuring the effects of our efforts.

Before I get too far into measurement, as a tech guy I have to make a distinction between KPIs and maintenance/performance metrics, because as I touched on earlier in this chapter, many people use these terms interchangeably, but they are fundamentally different. The following defines how they differ:

- A KPI is a specific, measurable target you set to track progress toward one of your significant business goals, like a 20% reduction in reactive maintenance. When you hit it you know your activities are achieving the outcomes you want.
- A metric is a raw data point measuring the performance or progress in a particular activity, such as the number of preventive maintenance jobs completed last month. It may not always be linked with a specified target.

The difference is basically strategic versus tactical. A KPI is like a headlight shining on your destination way up the road. Metrics are small signposts along that road telling you how far you have to go, when to take a turn, and alerting you to hazards in the road that might slow your progress toward reaching the end.

As someone who started out in supply chain management and gravitated toward facilities management, I operate from a categorical mindset (aka taxonomy). So instead of simply pointing out the KPIs and metrics that are high on my list,

I will present them in categories. Near the end of the chapter I will present metrics that are specific to an effective vendor management program.

KPIs and Metrics for Facilities

Safety Incidents

I put this KPI, which may be better suited as a category better be called a KPI category, at the top of my list because of the high degree of risk it presents to the organization and the amount of consideration and care it commands every minute in a facility's operations. Whether we are talking about an employee, a contracted vendor, or a customer of the facility, they must all be kept safe and aware that we are taking steps to protect them from harm. Because of the complexity of this KPI it is best considered to have multiple subcategories; however you might want to break them out as you wish and call them what you like. The following are some of those:

- *Customer Safety Incidents*: As the name presents, these are injuries or illnesses to customers associated with visiting the facility. In the healthcare space, again, there is that *extra layer of burden*—the patient. As most people are aware of or have experienced, in our healthcare facilities we don't let a discharged patient walk out of the facility on their own, regardless of their condition. They sit in a wheelchair until we get them to the curb, even if they could have sprinted there on their own. I know it's annoying, but that's the way it has to be. In healthcare facilities, especially in clinic environments, statistically we have a much higher percentage of people who are in frail condition, so our awareness and mitigation of hazards in the environment must be heightened.

- *Total Recordable Injury Frequency Rate*: This common KPI measures the number of work-related incidents that require medical attention or time away from work, divided by the total hours worked, providing a benchmark for overall safety performance within a facility. This is not only important to measure with our own facilities staff and the people who occupy our buildings, but also with our vendors. The safety record of vendors is a key consideration in whether we continue to keep them on or contract with them in the first place.
- *Lost Time Injury Frequency Rate*: This keeps track of the number of lost-time injuries per million hours worked. With our own employees the focus here is intently on the more severe incidents that impact productivity. With vendors, a high number here is a deal-breaker.
- *Fatalities*: This is also definitely a deal-breaker, unless there is a very good explanation.
- *Related safety data points*: Other data points for our employees and those of our vendors may include near miss rate, incident severity rate, safety audit compliance rate, and employee safety training completion rate.

User Satisfaction

Getting a handle on this KPI measure is tricky because the users of our facilities can encompass a wide range. Consider the healthcare environment, and say you are a COO of a multi-hospital system. The users your Facilities operation serves can include your own employees, contracted physicians and other healthcare workers, patients, and patients' families as well. So if you are running Facilities you might say you're serving not only your internal and external customers, but you are also serving your internal and external customers' customers. It can make your head spin trying to find out what they all think about your facilities from all of their disparate perspectives.

User satisfaction metrics in facilities management track the satisfaction levels of occupants, tenants, and visitors are with services, maintenance, and general condition of the facilities we manage. These typically are assessed through several vehicles, including feedback forms and surveys, or other methods—measuring cleanliness and comfort, maintenance response times, and overall functionality of the various spaces within a building.

Luckily for us in healthcare, the industry lives and dies by the patient, so a broad range of customer (think user) satisfaction data is collected, some of which encompasses facilities-related metrics. This kind of organization-wide cooperation on user satisfaction is also common in other industries; retail is one that quickly comes to mind. This kind of collaboration is another good argument for integration across all departments, even beyond the facilities-related business units.

Hospital Consumer Assessment of Healthcare Providers and Systems (HCAHPS) is a standardized survey used in the U.S. healthcare system to measure patients' perceptions of their hospital experience. Developed by the Centers for Medicare & Medicaid Services in partnership with the Agency for Healthcare Research and Quality, HCAHPS collects data on key aspects of hospital care, such as communication with nurses and doctors, responsiveness of hospital staff, cleanliness, and overall patient satisfaction.

Hospitals' HCAHPS scores impact their Medicare reimbursement through the value-based purchasing program, making patient experience a critical factor in healthcare quality and financial performance.

User satisfaction metrics are crucial not only for the success of our facility-management operations, but for the wider organization's positive reputation, ability to grow customer bases and to attract and retain tenants.

Asset Management Metrics

This category of KPIs/metrics measures the efficiency and effectiveness of our assets, which include not only the assets within our facilities but the buildings themselves as an asset. They help us keep a handle on asset condition, use, maintenance and reliability. They include:

- *Equipment Downtime*: When equipment in your facility is not operational because of repairs, maintenance, or breakdowns, it is unavailable for use. Whether planned or unplanned, equipment downtime can result in decreased customer satisfaction, heightened safety issues, and loss of revenue. Aside from helping managers improve operational efficiency and avoid downtime, monitoring this KPI gives them data that can help them identify recurring issues with specific pieces of equipment, different brands/models, or specific vendors/suppliers associated with providing or maintaining that equipment. Related measures are Mean Time Between Failures, Mean Time to Repair, and Planned Maintenance Percentage.
- *Planned versus Reactive Maintenance versus Emergency Ratio*: Simply put, this is the ratio of prevention to correction that goes on in your facilities. This KPI demonstrates the value that I mentioned earlier of having

engineers on your facilities team that can turn wrenches. It is also a key part of your asset management program, which I will detail below. Obviously, a higher rate of scheduled preventive maintenance tasks versus reactive tasks is preferred. If your numbers begin to trend toward more reactive or emergency tasks, you know you have a problem.

- *Overall Facility Uptime*: This is simply a measure of the percentage of time that our critical systems are able to be operational when they are needed.
- *Total Facilities Management Costs*: Calculating the total costs of maintaining a facility or complex divided by its square footage allows managers to compare maintenance costs among various facilities to reduce costs and improve operations.
- *Maintenance Costs Per Square Foot*: This is a simple yet valuable tool for comparing maintenance costs among multiple facilities, especially when you have many that have similar functions, such as my 285-clinic example. In this metric we include both proactive and reactive maintenance.
- *Utility Costs Per Square Foot*: Similar to the preceding KPI, this measure allows managers to compare utility costs among different facilities and during different time periods. It is valuable for tracking and improving utility cost-effectiveness. Again, this relates to utility expenses being a sign of a failing asset, resulting in variable or fluctuating costs.
- *Spare Parts Turnover Rate*: This is one KPI that demonstrates the importance of the marriage between Supply Chain and Facilities. It measures how frequently the inventory of spare parts in a facility is used and replenished. The pace at which parts are consumed and replaced reflects the efficiency of the facility's spare parts

management system asset item master, with a higher turnover rate indicating that parts are used regularly, and that active management of stock is occurring, which prevents overstocking or shortages. This relates to controlling costs related to assets, minimizing equipment and facility downtime, and optimizing inventory management (aka, "par levels").

- *Preventive Maintenance Compliance*: This can be thought of as either a KPI or a metric, as it measures how well a single facility or complex follows the plan for its preventive maintenance schedule. The measurement method can be as simple as a digital check-off list that is embedded in the CMMS. Lack of adherence to the schedule often becomes evident in increases in expensive breakdowns, reactive maintenance, equipment downtime, and even facility downtime depending on how critical the piece of equipment is to the operation of the facility.
- *Space Utilization Rates*: By measuring the occupied space in a facility versus the total available space, we can identify opportunities for how we efficiently utilize our spaces, including optimizing, allocating or repurposing, expanding or downsizing, and even decommissioning. Supply Chain is one area in which keeping a handle on the efficiency of space utilization is particularly valuable especially when creating requests for proposal (RFPs) for supplier category bid packages. For example, in a janitorial RFP you do not want to include the total square feet of a real estate property. Why? Not all of the square footage is utilized or "cleanable." By not backing out non-utilized square footage you are inflating your janitorial scheduled cleaning costs and ad-hoc floor care cleaning separate costs.

KPIs and Metrics for the Vendor Management Program

Most organizations have very poorly run and inconsistent vendor management programs, if they have one at all. It's just a fact. But again, if you don't put in significant time on the front end, I guarantee you will put in significantly more time cleaning up behind your lack of preparation, and paying a financial price for it.

In organizations with high-performing IFM systems, the vendor management program is communicated as a point of governance and ownership. It is also written into the service line agreements—those exhibits that are written into the contracts by Facilities after the master service agreement that Supply Chain owns. I see the vendor management program as the rules of engagement for those who want to participate, and I want to make sure that current and prospective vendors see it that way too.

To set up these rules of engagement we have a system of measurement with its own set of metrics that relate to our expectations for those who want to do business with, are doing business with, or would like to continue doing business with, our IFM system. These measures relate to:

- Assuring performance and quality
- Minimizing risk
- Maintaining healthy vendor relationships

We start with assessing how well the job is consistently done.

Gauging and Ensuring Vendor Performance and Quality

Earlier I addressed self-performance and my definition of gearing ratios—the percentage of wrench-turning done by our own people versus outside contractors. Within that we should expect vendors to perform at the same high level as we demand from our employees. In addition to some of the performance metrics I detailed above that measure the performance of both, we look at a few of the following extras from our vendors:

Vendor Compliance Score: This KPI measures the vendor's adherence to industry standards, legal regulations, and contractual obligations. I won't go into how I arrive at this score numerically, but the metrics involved include: compliance with regulatory requirements, including safety, financial, and sustainability/environmental; the number of audits and inspections passed or failed; and the percentage of contracts in which the vendor received penalties for non-compliance.

On-Time Delivery (OTD) Rate: This KPI, which is also relevant to Supply Chain in the IFM, measures the vendor's ability to meet agreed-upon delivery schedules. The key metrics for OTD are percentage of on-time deliveries, average delay time per delivery, and frequency of late deliveries. Again, I won't go into what my tolerances are for these metrics; that depends on what you are willing to accept in your facilities and asset management systems.

Quality Performance: Our Quality Performance KPI tracks another aspect of quality—the level of defects in both products and delivery of service. The metrics gauged for meeting this KPI are defect rate (per unit or service), number of product recalls or instances of rework, and the number of customer complaints or returns. On that last part, the seriousness of the customer complaints can also be an issue, though that can be a subjective measure.

Vendor Performance Index: This KPI is an overall score of vendor performance that considers multiple factors, including quality, price, service, and delivery. Important metrics for developing such an index include an aggregate score from multiple KPIs, including OTD, quality, and cost control; consistency of performance over time, and ability to meet all aspects of the service line agreements.

Assessing and Managing Risk in the Vendor Management Program

I assess and manage risk in an IFM system through the use of a vendor risk scorecard. This tool—part of any effective vendor management program—evaluates potential risks vendors might pose. Factors involved include contract-related risks, cybersecurity risks, level of financial health, and their active efforts to mitigate risk.

In addition to some key KPIs I covered before the vendor management section that are applicable to both vendors and staff (e.g., injuries and workplace safety), the following are other critical KPIs and scorecards that can help evaluate vendor risk:

Contract Risk and Liability: This KPI evaluates the level of risk associated with vendor contracts, including legal, financial, and reputational risks. Important issues include the number of clauses that protect the vendor company, including those for indemnity and insurance coverage; length of contract and termination clauses; and any history of disputes or litigation with the vendor.

Cybersecurity Risk: This KPI mainly involves information technology vendors, but it can concern any vendor that shares digital information with your systems. It measures the vendor's ability to protect your organization's data and prevent cyber threats. Key metrics include the number of security breaches or incidents attributed to the vendor; vulnerabilities or weaknesses identified in third-party audits; and the vendor's adherence to security frameworks, such as the NIST Cybersecurity Framework and ISO 27001.

Diversity Profile: The Diversity Profile provides a comprehensive assessment of an organization's commitment to fostering an inclusive and equitable workplace. This rating is based on multiple diversity dimensions, including workforce composition (representation across gender, race, ethnicity, and other demographics), inclusive hiring and promotion practices, supplier diversity, and leadership diversity. It also considers the organization's policies on equity, inclusion training, employee resource groups, and overall commitment to creating a diverse and inclusive culture.

Environmental, Social, and Governance (ESG)/ Sustainability/GREEN Profile: The ESG Sustainability Profile provides a comprehensive assessment of an organization's ESG impact. This rating is based on multiple sustainability dimensions, including environmental performance (carbon footprint, resource efficiency, and waste management), social responsibility (labor practices, diversity, and community engagement), and governance factors (ethics, transparency, and regulatory compliance). It also considers the organization's sustainability commitments, risk mitigation strategies, and long-term ESG resilience.

Employee Turnover Rate: Not only an important indicator in our own enterprise, it is also a vital metric to monitor for our vendors. While this is a challenging metric to get eyes on, with some vendors we can get a sense of it from industry news or from the observations of our internal teams.

Financial Stability: This KPI assesses the vendor's financial health to gauge the risk of them going out of business or facing financial instability. Important metrics to consider for this KPI are widely recognized measures of financial health, including credit rating or financial scoring, debt-to-equity ratios, profitability margins, payment terms, and outstanding invoices.

Risk Mitigation Planning: This evaluates how well the vendor has prepared for potential disruptions or crises (e.g., supply chain disruptions and natural disasters). Key measures include existence of a documented business continuity plan, demonstrated ability to recover from past disruptions, and documented regular review and updates of contingency plans.

Supply Chain Resilience: This KPI measures how effectively the vendor manages its own supply chain to ensure continuity of service. Metrics include diversification of suppliers and sourcing, lead times and impact of supply chain disruptions, and percentage of critical components with single-source suppliers.

Vendor Risk Profile: This is a comprehensive view we can develop of the vendor's overall risk factors. This rating is based on multiple risk dimensions, including financial, operational, and geopolitical factors; risk-adjusted performance over time; and risk mitigation measures currently in place (insurance, hedging, etc.).

Assessing Customer Satisfaction and the Vendor Relationship

The key to any successful vendor management program is a strong relationship between the IFM system and its vendors. This relationship, as in any, is based on maintaining two-way satisfaction between the parties. The following are two important ratings related to the relationship:

Vendor Relationship Management: This KPI measures current vendors on the quality of their relationship with the IFM entity, which can impact cooperation, innovation, and collaboration. Several factors are tracked with current vendors. These include frequency of communication and meetings, level of collaboration on new initiatives or improvement and vendor satisfaction scores from internal teams.

Customer Satisfaction/Net Promoter Score. This KPI can be used with current and prospective vendors. It assesses the vendor's relationship with their own customers, which can reflect on their reliability and performance. Key metrics include the net promoter score from the vendor's customers, the vendor's overall reputation in the market, and feedback or satisfaction surveys from internal teams.

This list may seem exhaustive, but by monitoring the foregoing KPIs, you can more comprehensively assess and manage vendors across a wide range of factors. This information is critical when we start looking at rationalizing and optimizing, as part of the vendor management program. When I come into an organization, these processes start with what I call vendor forensics.

Optimization and Rationalization Starts with Vendor Forensics

Some people call it diagnostics. I like the word forensics because it's like a crime scene. You need to investigate and then do your due diligence. You are mostly trying to get at this question: How many like vendors do I have that are doing like services?

Say I come into a company and do a little digging, and I find that they have 80 janitorial companies out of their 200 buildings. Believe me, numbers like that are not uncommon in my experience. Why would they do that? It makes absolutely no sense. This indicates that to me immediately their contracts and pricing and terms are going to be all over the board. No consistency. No standards.

Out of those 80 vendors, I'm going to knock that number down to maybe five. When they do that, they will absolutely save money. Period. They will also greatly reduce their risk, because their contracts, especially the master service agreement, will be standardized. Pricing will be consistent. Scope of work will be consistent. This is what we call rationalization.

Another term in facilities, often confused with rationalization, is optimization. The two are very different. Optimization is what you are doing when you put in place consistent pricing, standards and scopes of work that make up the exhibits in your service line agreements.

Together, rationalization and optimization combine in your vendor management program to create operational efficiencies. If you have 80 different vendors providing janitorial services among 285 clinics in seven states, you have an unmanageable abundance of contracts. That is why decentralization often translates into uncontrollable costs and uncontrollable measurements. It's impossible. So just to say one vendor is better than another is not fact-based. It must be based on the metrics, and their performance against those metrics. Vendors can then be measured contractually based on a defined scope of work, pricing, and performance of the service level agreement. Only then can we compare one vendor against another to improve outcomes going forward.

We continue with this theme as we move on to Supply Chain.

Chapter 5

Supply Chain Operations: Integrating Facilities Management with Procurement

It's critical that we drive digitization of supply chains, because without it, there will be no transparency; and without transparency, there will be no accountability.

–Christian Lanng

Supply Chain Operations and Integrated Facilities Management (IFM)

In Chapter 2 I noted that top executive management in an organization needs to set up clear business rules based on Responsible, Accountable, Consulted and Informed (RACI), defining ownership and accountability in IFM. I also insisted

 DOI: 10.4324/9781003773955-6

that within those business rules, the row on the RACI chart titled, "Master Service Agreements" (MSAs) should indicate that Supply Chain is *Responsible*. That means Supply Chain owns the MSAs that are central to the organization's vendor management program. The problem, in my experience, is that most organizations are not operating under a formal vendor management program, at least not a singular one that all the departments/business units concerned with facilities management are aligned around.

In many organizations I have seen it's common for Facilities to do entire contracts on their own in the absence of an enterprise-wide MSA. That's a problem, because having scattershot, poorly written agreements puts organizations, along with the people that walk into their facilities, at a high level of risk.

Why would these agreements not be written by the people—in Supply Chain—who are most adept at writing solid contracts?

The answer is usually that they're too busy. Take a hospital system, for example, in which Supply Chain's biggest contracts are procurement in the medical realm, with umbrella categories such as cardiovascular, imaging, and/or pharmaceutical, that are huge and complicated. If the organization's procurement is not contracted out to a group purchasing organization (GPO) the Supply Chain people are busy day, day in and day out with their own in-house supplier management. They simply don't have the time, so they typically don't support Facilities because they don't have enough people.

But if all of the leaders in the organization were thinking strategically with a supply chain/procurement mindset, they would have everything bucketed by categories ranked by severity and importance. Think of it: A non-functioning smoke alarm installed by a Facilities employee can be just as deadly to a patient as a faulty pacemaker implanted by a surgeon, and just as costly in a lawsuit, so Facilities and Supply Chain need to be joined at the hip.

Again, everyone wants to do right thing, but that often doesn't happen, because people get too busy. Even in the midst of all of that there needs to be an organization-wide mindset that appreciates the concept that putting in a considerable amount of work on the front end *always* decreases the amount of work going forward. So however "busy" we are now, if we don't invest that upfront extra time to decrease our overall time, we will just cause more work for ourselves down the line.

Synergy Between Procurement and Facilities: Optimizing Vendor Relationships

Beyond creating the master vendor service agreement portions of the Facilities contracts and lending further expertise to Facilities in creating their service line agreements, Supply Chain professionals play an important role with regard to Facilities—doing what most people would consider their "usual job."

In that traditional role, Supply Chain professionals ensure efficient, cost-effective procurement, storage, and delivery of goods and services. In the context of their place in IFM, they accomplish these things in support of everything needed for facility operations, maintenance, and upgrades, except when it comes to services; Facilities covers most services through their vendor agreements.

As you might guess, going back to Chapter 3, all of this Supply Chain activity in support of Facilities ultimately impacts operational efficiency and realized cost savings.

Facilities can do a masterful job of optimizing its vendor agreements and cutting down on costs for operations, maintenance, and upgrades, but if Supply Chain doesn't do the same due diligence with its suppliers, unnecessarily high costs and operational disruptions can be passed on to Facilities and thus to the entire enterprise. This can happen when deficiencies occur in several areas of Supply Chain responsibility shown below:

1. ***Supplier Relationship Management:*** Just as with Facilities vendor relationship management I presented in the previous chapter, Supply Chain managers must nurture robust relationships with suppliers, negotiating strong contracts, ensuring quality, and creating a framework for quick resolution when issues arise.
2. ***Risk Management:*** Through the master service agreements that they develop themselves and for Facilities, they identify and mitigate potential risks, including supply and transportation disruptions.
3. ***Logistics and Transportation:*** Movement of goods and materials to and from the facility must be optimized to minimize costs and ensure timely delivery.
4. ***Cost Savings:*** Supply Chain managers should constantly strive to make efficiency gains, negotiate better prices, and implement other cost-saving measures.
5. ***Procurement:*** Supply Chain managers must aggressively rationalize and optimize suppliers for sourcing and purchasing the necessary materials and equipment for facility maintenance, repairs, and upgrades.
6. ***Inventory Management:*** Inventory levels must be effectively managed to ensure essential supplies are readily available, while preventing stockouts and minimizing storage costs.

7. ***Data Analysis and Reporting:*** Supply Chain managers must track and intensively analyze their own supply chain key performance indicators (KPIs) to continuously improve operations improvement, and provide reports to stakeholders which include various IFM management teams. Many of these metrics overlap with Facilities interests.

Supply Chain can go a step farther by helping Facilities with vendor management. Now, they aren't necessarily well-versed in the world of facilities-related vendors, nor should they be expected to have that level of knowledge. But just change *vendor* management to their vernacular of *supplier* management, and you find a place where experienced Supply Chain professionals have some admirable skills.

Again, people are busy, and you might find it unreasonable to expect Facilities and Supply Chain personnel to devote considerable time working collaboratively, but I implore you to look back at that list above. Then let me repeat the theme I will keep harping on throughout this book: However "busy" we might be, if we don't invest extra time up front to decrease our overall time, we will cause more work for ourselves down the line.

Helping to Manage Vendor Master and Service Line Agreements

In the previous chapter I explored vendor agreements—the comprehensive contracts defining the business terms between an organization and its suppliers/vendors for purchasing goods or services. In Chapter 2 I also detailed where the overlap exists between Supply Chain and Facilities in these. Now I want to present some of the collaborative aspects that affect not only the health of the IFM ecosystem within an organization, but the health of the entire enterprise.

Let's look at some of the elements involved with managing our agreements and relationships with entities outside of our organizations.

- Any successful relationship requires frequent attention and active support. Periodic reviews of vendor agreements are vital to our vendor management program and vendor relationship management. These reviews involve scrutinizing pricing, payment terms, delivery schedules, and quality standards to ensure they meet the organization's needs and provide value. Reviewing agreements regularly can lead to renegotiations for better terms or compliance with new regulations, which enhance vendor relationships and cost efficiencies.
- Agreements often include clauses for volume discounts, payment terms, and warranties. Legal and procurement teams typically collaborate to ensure our organizations' interests are protected by our contracts.
- In the previous chapter I noted that service level agreements, performance metrics, and KPIs are often embedded in these agreements for continual evaluation. Regular audits of vendor compliance with performance and financial indicators can lead to cost savings, quality improvement, and time savings.
- Contract lifecycle management helps in tracking renewals, amendments, and terminations. Insights from these agreements can inform strategic sourcing initiatives in Supply Chain, which helps maintain a balanced supply chain and minimizes risk from supplier dependency.

The Role of Strategic Sourcing and Category Management in IFM

Successful supply chain operations require professionals who are adept at strategic sourcing and category management. In Supply Chain, where I originally started in the facilities industry, we spend a lot of time talking about what I call "… ization" words. The biggest of those in supplier management are categorization, rationalization, and optimization. Facilities personnel would do well by learning about these three "… izations" from their Supply Chain partners in the organization.

Categorization is obvious. In Supply Chain, categorization often called "taxonomy"—which is part of optimization—entails putting products into categories, as we do in Facilities with vendors. The suppliers of those products may overlap in different categories. The other two terms are not as obvious. As I touched on earlier, while both "rationalization" and "optimization" are used in supplier management, and they are related, they are two different animals. Let me explain a little further:

- *Rationalization* focuses foremost on reducing the number of suppliers by eliminating those that are either underperforming or redundant. This helps streamline the supply base.
- *Optimization* goes beyond just reducing the number of suppliers to a more comprehensive analysis that seeks to ensure the remaining suppliers are performing at their highest level. Factors in this evaluation include quality, cost, responsiveness, and more.

Essentially, the goal of rationalization is to reduce the number of suppliers in a supply management program to reduce costs, elevate efficiency, and strengthen relationships between suppliers and the organization. Optimization seeks to refine the supply base, which may also mean removing more suppliers from the list if needed. To put this in a Facilities context, anywhere you see the word "suppliers" in the definitions above, you generally can replace that with the word "vendors."

Say you have 80 fire life and safety vendors. You're seeking to rationalize that down to a handful. Optimization correlates with that to the extent that it means while you're optimizing cost, you're also optimizing the performance of vendors based on their scopes of work. So they overlap somewhat, but they have distinct differences.

Good supply chain people are adept at rationalization and standardization, but that is for the areas they understand. They may thoroughly appreciate how my Facilities-related vendor bid template works to rationalize and optimize, but they don't have a complete understanding of the differences in my categories of vendors. They would not be able to send out a thorough bid for janitorial or HVAC, even though they "get" my bid template. A Facilities professional has the advantage of being expert in the nuances of those specialties.

This goes back to my 70% | 30% generalization in Chapter 2. In that 30% that consists of your contract exhibits—the service line agreement—is where you need the expert to contribute. The supply chain person knows how to create ironclad contracts, requests for proposal (RFPs), and group bids. Remember, going back to RACI, experienced Supply Chain managers are geniuses at cost reduction and risk mitigation, and RFPs/group bids are all about those two things.

This means Supply Chain needs to have at least Consulted roles on the RACI chart when we are looking at RFPs/group bids anywhere throughout the IFM enterprise. They can help you prevent financial jeopardy because they're controlling that cost through better written bids and contracts. They're reducing risk because they're writing the structured terms and conditions. So they're reducing organizational risk incurred overall. So to conclude, Supply Chain should be an instrument to do what most in Facilities and/or Construction don't always know how to do, and that's rationalizing like services through group bids.

Exploring the Nature of Supply Chain/Facilities Collaboration

As I noted in Chapters 2 and 4, in a perfect world, Supply Chain and Facilities work together, coordinating the flow of within and among various facilities, and collaborating on optimizing space, meeting maintenance needs, and managing inventory. Much of this is accomplished by sharing data that is integrated between them, so they are always ready to adjust in real time to ensure efficient operations across the entire IFM enterprise.

With ownership of the master service agreement in Facilities and Construction, Supply Chain sets the stage and the tone for vendor management programs. But in IFM Utopia outside of the MSAs, they are also helping educate as part of their ownership. They should help define vendor management for other departments. They don't have to always lead it, because again, they're busy, but they should set the tone and an example what a quarterly business line review should look like.

Just as in Facilities in the previous chapter, we use an extensive list of KPIs to track and validate supply chain performance. One of the most widely used lists of KPIs in healthcare supply chain comes from the Association for Health Care Resource & Materials Management of the American Hospital Association. This list of 32 essential KPIs is shown in Table 5.1.

In their insightful 2024 book titled, *Advancing Strategic Sourcing and Healthcare Affordability: Our Discovery of the Lacuna Triangle* authors Michael Georgulis and Mark West noted that all of these KPIs are "essential and highly valuable for measuring supply chain operations." I agree. They added, however, that when it comes to true strategic sourcing there are "two glaring categories of omission." I have written at length so far in this book and will write much more about these two missing pieces: realized cost savings and employee experience and development.

Table 5.1 AHRMM Key Performance Indicators

Finance	Supply Accounts Payable
	Supply Expense Per Case Mix Index Adjusted Discharge
	Supply Expense as Percent of Net Revenue
	Spend Under Management
	Inventory Turns
	Supply Chain Labor Expense Per Case Mix Index Adjusted Discharge
Operations	Perfect Order
	Total Suppliers Per $1M Non-Labor Supply Expense
	Percentage of Purchase Order Lines with Expedited Shipping Costs
	Supply Chain FTEs Per $1M in Total Non-Labor Supply Expense

(Continued)

Table 5.1 (Continued)

Patient Safety	Expired Products as a Percentage of Total Number of On-Hand Products in Inventory Recall Management – Closed Volume Percentage Rate Recall Management – Delayed Recalls Percentage Rate
Resiliency	Internal Requisition and Order Fill Percentage Rate Primary Distributor Backorder Percentage Rate Percentage of Items Stored in the Item Master with Identified Substitutes Primary Distributor Fill Percentage Rate Non-Labor Supply Expense Per Case Mix Index (CMI) Adjusted Patient Days (APD)
Data Standards	Percentage of Invoice Lines Received with a Global Trade Identification Number (GTIN) Percentage of Invoice Lines Received with a Global Location Number (GLN) Percentage of Items Stored in the Item Master Populated with a GTIN Percentage of Purchase Order Lines Sent Out with a GTIN Percentage of Items Stored in the Item Master Populated with a GLN
Environmental Sustainability	EPP Products as a Percentage of Total Office Supply Expense Recycled Products as a Percentage of Total Printing and Copier Paper Expense Percentage of Medical Supplies That are Reprocessed Linen Pounds Per Adjusted Patient Day Copy/Print Page Volumes Per Employee Waste Pounds Per Adjusted Patient Day

Source: Association for Health Care Resource & Materials Management. 2023. AHRMM Keys for Supply Chain Excellence. www.ahrmm .org /keys).

One of the major barriers to getting a comprehensive view of realized cost savings in Supply Chain, especially in the healthcare industry, is the presence, or maybe better to say the omnipresence, of GPOs.

Group Purchasing Organizations: Go or No Go?

GPOs are commonly used for procurement of supplies and services in many class-of-trade industries. This is especially prevalent in the healthcare industry, where more than 95% of hospitals are affiliated with at least one GPO (Dean et al., 2024).

GPOs aggregate purchasing volume from their member organizations and use that leverage to negotiate discounts with manufacturers, distributors and other vendors. Let's first look at the benefits for procurement and Supply Chain operations and then look at the cons, particularly when it comes to using GPOs in Facilities and Construction.

Understanding the Pros of Group Purchasing Organizations

A GPO leverages its members' collective buying power to negotiate discounts with suppliers for goods and services. GPOs are particularly useful in sectors such as healthcare, where they can negotiate for medical equipment, supplies, pharmaceuticals, or food, achieving better pricing than individual institutions could. Members of GPOs benefit from reduced costs, standardized purchasing procedures, and access to a broader selection of suppliers.

GPOs often provide members with pre-negotiated contracts, which simplifies procurement time invested in writing their own internal master service agreements, negotiating pricing, and time invested in market research. They help in managing supply chain risks by securing supply agreements. Compliance with industry standards and regulations is facilitated through GPO frameworks. GPOs can offer access to exclusive deals or innovations not available on the open market. They promote economies of scale, which can lead to significant cost savings and price protection. Membership in a GPO can also enhance supplier relationships and service quality.

Understanding the Cons of Using GPOs for Construction and Facilities Management

GPOs can influence facilities management in two primary ways: indirectly, by managing significant portions of the supply chain's procurement, contracting, and operational functions; or directly, when engaged by Facilities departments to oversee vendor relationships for purchasing and maintenance services. While some organizations may choose not to involve GPOs at all, it's important to consider the potential drawbacks of integrating them into the IFM environment.

GPO contracts for services are often considered "cloud-based contracting"—they typically offer percentage-based discounts rather than itemized or fixed pricing. Because of their typical operational framework they must write "umbrella contracts" that meet the needs of everyone and that's why they commonly put language typically in every GPO contract that they allow for local negotiations, because they know that a carte blanche umbrella contract will not result in the most favored pricing. This makes it difficult to assess cost savings or compare against baselines, especially for project work. GPO master agreements in Construction and Facilities often lack detailed, industry-specific scopes of work.

One crucial difference between an IFM service provider and a GPO is that an IFM provider is physically in your building and managing the day-to-day operations of a client, and they have people in there. GPOs do not manage the daily operational aspects of Facilities, including issues such as vendor no-shows or late arrivals, underperformance by vendors and suppliers, and discrepancies in invoicing and billing, which are often permitted when a portion of the contract can be left open for "local contract negotiations." They do not actively manage or resolve many of the routine, on-the-ground issues across various vendors, services, and categories.

While GPOs can support procurement at a basic level, they often fall short in meeting the real-world demands of facilities management. Their teams—often coming from clinical or healthcare backgrounds—typically lack the operational experience, risk awareness, and technical understanding required in this field. Unlike dedicated facilities engineers, GPOs rarely offer standardized contracts tailored to facilities' specific needs.

Moreover, GPOs are not equipped to provide professional guidance on staff augmentation models or labor-to-task gearing ratios. They also tend to lack meaningful expertise in areas such as property management and real estate strategy.

This gap highlights the essential role of Facilities professionals, whose contributions extend well beyond procurement to ensure safety, compliance, operational performance, and long-term asset stewardship.

Conclusion

For Supply Chain and Facilities teams to truly align, they must understand each other's priorities, constraints, and areas of expertise. Supply Chain can strengthen contract development but often lacks nuanced knowledge of the vendor landscape, especially across the varied domains of facilities management at local, regional, and global levels. Without that context, contracts may satisfy technical specs yet fall short in securing the most suitable service partners.

When both teams collaborate early—developing detailed, service-specific scopes of work and distinguishing essential providers from optional ones—they can drive smarter sourcing decisions and build stronger, more integrated vendor relationships.

That's where the collaboration deepens. As a subject matter expert in their industry, Facilities is informing Supply Chain of what they need to know about Facilities vendors in order to go out to bid. That's where the *marriage* comes in to create a stronger union between contracts to support the facility engineers and minimize risk. Again, this union requires defined vendor and supplier management programs that all vendors and suppliers must adhere to, prior to successfully obtaining a company contract to deliver products and services.

Now we move on to Construction and Real Estate, the business units that manage our biggest assets—the buildings that house our operations.

References

Dean, E. B., Pierre, R., Carter, S., & Bond, A. M. (2024). Role of supply chain intermediaries in steering hospital product choice: Group purchasing organizations and biosimilars. *Health Affairs Scholar, 2*(6), qxae067. https://doi.org/10.1093/haschl/qxae067.

Georgulis Jr., M., & West, M. C. (2024). *Advancing strategic sourcing and healthcare affordability: Our discovery of the lacuna triangle*. Routledge, Taylor & Francis.

Chapter 6

Real Estate/ Construction: The Nuts and Bolts of Strategic Planning

You can use an eraser on the drafting table or a sledgehammer on the construction site.

–Frank Lloyd Wright

In this chapter we move first into Real Estate and then Construction, the remaining two traditional integrated facilities management (IFM) business units. These need to be taken together, because in these two departments is where we see the convergence of the C-suite and facilities management, driven by some of the most crucial strategic considerations of a health system—*capital planning and real estate portfolio management*. We start with Real Estate.

DOI: 10.4324/9781003773955-7

In true IFM there is a formal Real Estate Department, which is responsible—in alignment with executive management's overall organizational goals—for strategic planning, acquisition, and management of real estate assets. Real Estate's direction and responsibility begins at the top of the organization, especially in the ever-evolving healthcare industry, where merger and acquisition (M&A) activity, service expansion/redirection (think marketing and rebranding), and service contraction, are commonplace.

None of those things happen without intimate involvement of Real Estate/Construction, because these events involve commissioning, decommissioning, and renovating the organization's most expensive physical assets. Much of the strategic planning that takes place in Real Estate is long-term, and includes acquisition, disposition, renovation and leasing of facilities based on current and future business needs.

Capital Planning and Portfolio Management: Managing a Shifting Landscape

The facilities asset and real estate portfolio landscape in healthcare is always shifting, from the macro scale of multi-site acquisitions to the micro scale of adding a new outpatient surgery wing to an old hospital. On the macro scale, the industry is always on the move with M&A activity, regardless of whatever level of uncertainty is happening in the broader markets. Case in point: As I was writing this chapter in late April 2025, *Becker's Hospital Review* reported that in just the three months from January 1 to April 1 of 2025, 14 major M&As involving hospitals were finalized throughout the United States—ranging from single hospitals to a 56-hospital merger (Cass, 2025).

In this industry, strategic capital planning and portfolio management are central to the Real Estate business unit, driven not only by physical infrastructure needs but by deeper economic and demographic realities. Understanding the payer mix—Medicaid, Medicare, private insurance, and the uninsured—is essential, as it directly influences profitability, service planning, and facility allocation. Future growth strategies must align with shifting patient populations, care delivery models, and the rapid pace of technological advancement, ensuring that real estate assets remain adaptable and financially sustainable in a dynamic healthcare landscape.

A report from the American Hospital Association (AHA) titled, "The Cost of Caring: Challenges Facing America's Hospitals in 2025," (AHA, 2025) encapsulated what AHA described as a "perfect storm" of financial pressures currently facing health systems that includes:

- *Persistent Cost Growth*: This is driven in large part by labor costs associated with a community-anchored, highly-skilled/educated, and well-paid workforce in which most jobs are very difficult to outsource or automate.
- *Inadequate Reimbursement*: Medicare reimbursement in 2023 covered only 83 cents on every dollar hospitals spend, and while inflation rose 14.1% from 2022 to 2024, Medicare net inpatient rates increased by only 5.1%.
- *Hospital Expenses Outpace Inflation*: In 2024, overall inflation rose 2.9% while hospital expenses grew by 5.1%

One reason we have so many aging hospitals in healthcare is that they are too expensive to build. What once cost a few hundred million dollars to build from scratch is now a billion dollars or more. They are not only costly to maintain.

There is also another side to the cost of traditional hospitals that make them prohibitively expensive: They are a part of an equally aging paradigm of doing business in healthcare. The old fee-for-service model that mega-hospitals represent—treating sick people rather than keeping them well and out of the hospital—is not sustainable in the emerging healthcare landscape.

The trends in real estate portfolio management are moving toward finding financially sustainable platforms that improve access by meeting patients where they are, attending to their continuum of care, and lowering costs of care in the process. These trends reflect two of the major drivers in modern healthcare:

1. *Value-based Care*, succinctly defined as the overall cost of improving outcomes that are valued by patients and populations.
2. The globally adopted *Quintuple Aim* of Healthcare Improvement, the pillars of which are Patient Experience, Clinical Outcomes, Financial Sustainability, Clinician Well-being, and Health Equity.

Capital planning is the process of budgeting for and managing long-term investments in capital assets such as buildings, machinery, staffing at par levels, and technology to support future growth or operational efficiency. The process, done correctly, begins with some of the top considerations of the organization: the impact of capital investments on operational capabilities and market position, along with their alignment with the company's strategic plan and financial goals.

The capital planning process can be complex, including forecasting the financial needs for these investments, assessing performance of existing properties in the portfolio, and planning for funding source—whether they will be through debt, equity, or internal cash flows. That aspect of capital planning involves evaluating different funding options to minimize the cost of capital and maximize returns, while incorporating risk assessment to mitigate potential investment pitfalls.

Implementing the capital plan into action involves stakeholder engagement for alignment and buy-in. The boots-on-the ground aspects of the plan include ensuring that resources are allocated wisely to support strategic objectives while managing risks associated with large-scale capital investments. This includes lifecycle cost analysis to assess long-term asset sustainability. Regular reviews and adjustments to capital plans will always be necessary due to changing economic conditions.

In a large, dynamic healthcare organization, Real Estate/Construction teams know they'll be continuously involved in building, acquiring, or renovating facilities. Yet surprisingly, many organizations lack a truly strategic and collaborative approach to planning for these efforts—missing the opportunity to align Real Estate/Construction decisions with broader operational goals.

I often visit organizations managing dozens or even hundreds of facilities across the United States, yet when I ask, "Can I see your current capital master plan?" no one in Real Estate, Construction, or Facilities has a clear answer. Instead, I'm usually handed something incomplete—lacking detail, ownership clarity, and the practical tools that define roles, responsibilities, and execution guidelines.

You can't just buy buildings, or elevators, or HVAC systems in bulk and have them sitting around waiting for you when conditions say you need them. You also can't succeed in facilities management if you are making a series of knee-jerk reactions to the market. You must have a collaborative capital master plan that involves the C-suite, Finance, Real Estate, Construction, Facilities, and the Supply Chain.

Managing the Real Estate Portfolio

At the top of the list for Real Estate professionals is managing the organization's real estate portfolio. A real estate portfolio in the context of real estate investment is defined as a collection of properties owned or managed by an individual or corporation. This includes ensuring that the organization's needs for real estate are met, and identifying opportunities for optimization, such as space utilization and cost reduction.

Successful real estate portfolio management requires ongoing analysis to assess the performance of each property in terms of revenue, cost, occupancy rates, and market value. Portfolio managers utilize several metrics to evaluate performance, including:

- ***Capitalization Rate:*** Often called simply the cap rate, this metric assesses potential return based on income.
- ***Net Operating Income (NOI):*** In real estate, this is the income a property generates after you subtract all of your operating expenses (excluding financing costs and taxes). Some of the metrics I presented in Chapter 4 for asset management are useful in getting to the NOI.
- ***Return on Investment:*** This includes the overall return on the property, including financing (such as mortgages) and changes in the property's value.

For a given industry, such as healthcare or retail, or hospitality, some of the portfolio considerations are different from the real estate investing mindset. For example, in real estate investing, individuals often seek diversification across various types of real estate (e.g., a mix of residential, commercial, and industrial) because it generally reduces financial risk. In a particular industry, however, we are usually limited in seeking such diversification, because we have a set of particular uses in mind. In healthcare, our mix is divided among care environments, such as inpatient (or acute), post-acute, outpatient, rehabilitation, long-term care, etc.

Managing a real estate portfolio involves strategies for acquiring, maintaining, leasing, and disposing of properties to maximize returns and align with organizational investment goals. Economic trends, local market conditions, and zoning laws significantly affect the portfolio strategy. An effective Real Estate team also employs professionals adept at market research, who are constantly studying growth trends and staying on the lookout for possible locations for new facilities.

In healthcare facilities management environments, Real Estate managers are master planners, developing long-term healthcare facility plans that account for a range of issues, including the needs of patients, type of treatment and care which can vary widely with their condition, age, and the intensity of resources needed to serve them. Planning and development also include ensuring that healthcare facilities are designed to optimize patient care, workflow, and efficiency of staff.

All of it must be done with the satisfaction of both patients and staff top of mind (back to that Quintuple Aim), and one of it can be done without cooperation among all the business units tied to IFM.

Dual Approaches of the Real Estate Strategy: Investment and Property Management

Since we are addressing facilities management in the context of the healthcare industry here, let's consider this from a clinical point of view: where the Facilities Department is concerned with taking care of the nervous and circulatory systems of buildings, the Real Estate Department, in partnership with Construction, takes care of the bones and the skin. Table 6.1 shows an example Responsible, Accountable, Consulted, and Informed chart that shows overall responsibilities of the various IFM business units.

Real Estate in IFM should generally not be responsible for vendors/suppliers related to the physical facilities. While Construction, Facilities, and Supply Chain are involved with vendor and supplier contracting in IFM, Real Estate works on developing and negotiating lease contracts and then managing them, ensuring that risk is minimized, and terms are optimal for the organization.

Real Estate has related property owner (landlord) versus tenant (company) responsibilities, and shares these owned responsibilities with Facilities (e.g., when HVAC is the responsibility of the company) or Construction (e.g., when a

Table 6.1 RACI Chart of IFM Business Units

Deliverable						
Capital Budget Approval	A	C	C	C	C	C
Site Selection & Lease Execution	C	A/R	I	C	C	I
Construction Planning and Permits	I	C	A/R	C	I	C
Store/Site Buildout	I	C	A/R	C	I	C
Facilities Equipment Installation	C	I	C	A/R	I	I
IT Infrastructure Setup	C	I	C	C	I	A/R
Vendor Sourcing & Procurement	C	I	C	C	A/R	C
Asset Tagging and Inventory	I	I	C	C	A/R	C
Operational Readiness/Go-Live	C	C	C	A/R	C	C
Ongoing Maintenance/Facilities Mgmt	I	I	I	A/R	C	C
Cost Tracking & Variance Reporting	A/R	I	C	C	C	I

facility needs to be built, or another needs to be turned back to its original "shell" condition and configuration at the end of a lease).

Now let's look at how Real Estate works together with Construction to meet the strategic goals of the capital master plan and real estate portfolio management.

Construction: Where Challenges Are Overcome By Innovation

When we get into the facility planning and development aspects of the Real Estate business unit, that is where Construction and Real Estate must work seamlessly together. Real Estate oversees construction projects, whether they are new buildings, renovations, or expansions of existing facilities. They are not like an onsite construction manager, because Construction has their own. Instead, Real Estate ensures that the construction activities align with the capital planning and portfolio management objectives.

The size and professional makeup of a Real Estate/ Construction business unit in an IFM ecosystem varies widely—from sizable to skinny. In a lean organization it may consist of one person having responsibility over Real Estate and two being accountable for Construction. It all depends on the size of the orgaization and the scope of its activities in these areas.

If I am in a large health system with intensive construction activity I still may decide I want an architect on my team for the value of that professional's experience as a trusted adviser. Of course, if I'm still hiring architectural firms I would have to weigh the value of having that full-time employee (FTE) on the books 365 days a year.

More commonly, other organizations that have a high volume of moves, adds, and changes may have internal people working on their teams, but they still hire significant outside support and they manage those schedules. They hire true project managers and construction planners internally who determine the needs, specs, and requirements and then communicate and coordinate with the outside contractors. That's much different from having an architect on staff.

When you move into more of a greenfield situation—building structures and complexes from the ground up—that's different. Greenfield projects entail land acquisition and zoning. You still have zoning issues with tenant improvement, but it is not the same level. A new piece of land is a blank slate where leadership, Real Estate and Construction can take their creative vision wherever they want. A big problem with that though, as I touched on earlier, is the cost, but innovative solutions can be found when the IFM enterprise and the C-suite work together.

In Construction, no matter the scale of the job, the team works a little more independently regarding supplier/vendor management than you would see in Facilities or Supply Chain. They go out to bid and hire a general contractor, and then the contractor subcontracts out whoever will be performing the work. Construction can recommend certain installations of systems, manufacturers, and service providers. While Construction teams can recommend specific system installations, manufacturers, or service providers, the selection of subcontractors is typically at the discretion of the General Contractor. However, this autonomy can be limited when the Client enforces the use of preferred subcontractors—particularly those with an existing master service agreements (MSAs). In such cases, the MSA or contract scope will clearly define the level of client involvement and whether subcontractor approval is required.

Healthcare Construction on a Retail Foundation

Ironically, one of the growing trends in saving money in healthcare real estate and construction emerged during the COVID pandemic. Long before this event paralyzed the retail environment, traditional cornerstone department stores that often served as "anchors" for large shopping malls were starting to fail and began closing one by one.

Sears is an example. The venerable brand started closing their massive stores in 2018, a practice that snowballed after the company filed for bankruptcy in October 2018. COVID exacerbated this trend. During the pandemic and in its aftermath, a flood of big chain stores began to shutter their doors.

Although there are notable examples of health systems converting retail buildings into clinics before the pandemic, it was in the 2020s that the healthcare industry really took notice. And why not? Healthcare was already under pressure to adopt a retail mindset by increasing demand for outpatient services, and a retail real estate landscape was opening up before their eyes. It offered a lot of what healthcare needed—existing infrastructure, central locations in communities that lacked access to healthcare services, ample parking, facilities that were convenient to public transportation, and visibility that is hard to miss.

In November 2023, Cooper University Healthcare opened its campus in Moorestown, N.J., built on the bones of a closed former Sears store in the Moorestown Mall that had been vacant since the height of the pandemic in 2000. With three stories and 166,000 square feet, the state-of-the art medical facility on opening boasted not only primary care doctor's offices, but those of more than 26 specialties, nearly 100 exam rooms, concierge services and even a café. In 2024 the health system expanded the Moorestown Campus offerings with physical therapy, radiology, infusion services, radiation therapy, an outpatient surgery center, and Cooper and Inspira Neuroscience, which offers diagnosis and treatment of neurological conditions (Cooper University Health, 2023).

This $150 million Cooper Health project addresses the results that can be obtained in speed of construction and money savings in converting a retail space for healthcare purposes. The construction progress in these sites can be greatly accelerated, with site permits and zoning potentially taking much less time. A building with existing infrastructure for most purposes can also save significant utility and plumbing installation costs. There are, however, challenges to consider.

Considerations in Repurposing a Retail Environment

The experience of the Medical University of South Carolina in developing its West Ashley Medical Pavilion—opened in Charleston in 2020, and created out of a closed J. C. Penney store—points out some both advantages and technical challenges that can come with such a project. and it can be applicable to converting any large, sprawling building to a healthcare use—particularly medical office buildings/ambulatory surgery centers.

The university contracted with McMillan Pazdan Smith Architecture in Charleston, and one of its design principals, Aaron Jeffers, highlighted some of the solutions that had to be developed in creating this new center (Jeffers, 2022). These included:

Advantages and challenges in the building structure: Floor-to-floor heights that were five to six feet taller than in most medical office buildings allowed them to add above-ceiling water and electrical infrastructure as well as specialized operating room equipment without compressing space. However, they found that lowering the ceilings wasn't a good option in some places where people needed access to equipment that required easy access for regular maintenance.

Working within an existing footprint: Most medical office building are rectilinear—designed with straight lines and right angles—while big retail stores are huge squares. This created challenges in placing elevators and other vertical elements, and creating efficient patient and staff traffic flows. These buildings also have limited access to daylight, so designers had to use creative approaches to bringing in natural light.

Upgrading Plumbing and HVAC systems: When redesigning big box retail and grocery stores, HVAC systems will likely have to be completely redesigned from the retail paradigm of moving large volumes of air through large empty spaces to channeling it through a multitude of medical suites and rooms. Big retail stores also have very little plumbing whereas a medical office buildings with 100+ exam rooms have plumbing everywhere, requiring significant plumbing infrastructure upgrades.

In addition to the significant technical construction challenges mentioned above, Real Estate also has a big job on its hands in lease negotiations. The extent of other changes that need to be made to convert the space to healthcare uses can be massive, including radical additions to plumbing, electrical, med gas, and even reworking the slab and foundational elements (Albert, 2024).

Who should be responsible on the lease for which of these various changes? If we ever decide to terminate this lease, do we have to put everything back the way it was when J. C. Penney let go of it? Or a bigger question: Should we really be leasing? Whether it is a strip mall, an old supermarket, an abandoned former Rite Aid store, or that huge department store, well-reasoned capital planning and portfolio management may suggest that buying a building and then renovating makes the most sense. Do we have the cash on hand so we can capitalize and amortize this expense? Or do we need to retain the option to get out of this building in the distant future?

Conclusion

The preceding considerations present examples of how striving for effective IFM is an effort that profoundly affects the organization—from a CEO contemplating a merger to a Supply Chain worker procuring a critical HVAC component. Real Estate plays a unique role in minding any possible breaches in the IFM strategy, positioning it as a vital conduit for alignment and integration. This includes helping to facilitate strong collaboration and clear communication across all IFM stakeholders—which is the subject of our next chapter.

References

AHA. (2025, April 30). The cost of caring: Challenges facing America's hospitals in 2025. www.aha.org/costsofcaring.

Albert, J. (2024, March 26). Converting retail spaces into health care facilities. *HFM Magazine*. www.hfmmagazine.com/articles/4957-converting-retail-spaces-into-health-care-facilities.

Cass, A. (2025, April 25). 14 hospital M&As finalized in 2025. *Becker's Hospital Review*. www.beckershospitalreview.com/hospital-transactions-and-valuation/14-hospital-mas-finalized-in-2025/.

Cooper University Health. (2023). Cooper University Health Care's new Moorestown campus opens. https://blogs.cooperhealth.org/news/2023/11/cooper-university-health-cares-new-moorestown-campus-opens/.

Jeffers, A. (2022, April 25). Converting retail spaces to healthcare. Healthcare Design. https://healthcaredesignmagazine.com/trends/turning-to-empty-retail-spaces-to-fill-healthcare-demand/54111

Chapter 7

Enhancing Collaboration Within IFM

Talent wins games, but teamwork and intelligence win championships.

–Michael Jordan

Envisioning the Integrated Facilities Management (IFM) Collaborative

As I detailed in the previous chapter, strategic planning and portfolio management roles of Real Estate tie this business unit closely to the C-suite—not in political power, but in alignment to overarching organizational goals, necessitating robust collaboration and communication with all of the IFM stakeholders.

The concept of IFM should seen as a true *collaborative*, which is defined as "an organized group of people or entities who work in partnership toward a particular goal." Though

DOI: 10.4324/9781003773955-8

all of the entities have vital roles, Real Estate is the point at which information flows up and down throughout the IFM ecosystem.

Think of this collaborative as a pyramid, as shown in Figure 7.1. This pyramid is not a hierarchy of who is most important or powerful; rather, it represents how the mandate of our "extra layer of responsibility" for collaboration and communication in healthcare industry IFM flows from top leadership throughout the IFM enterprise.

When we look at IFM as a collaborative, the departmental silos melt away. As a niche IFM service provider I constantly hear department managers try to make the case for why

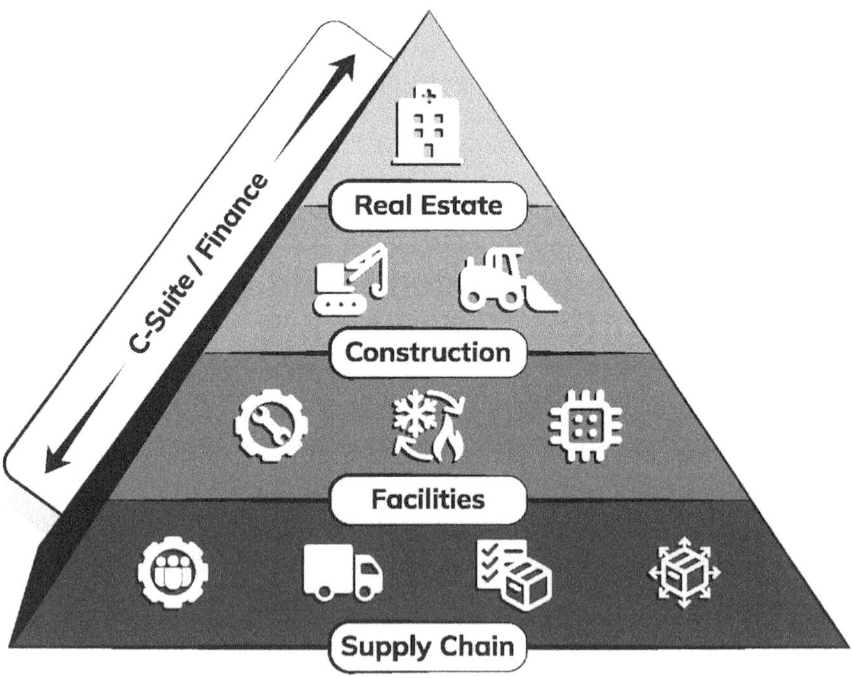

Figure 7.1 The integrated facilities management collaborative enterprise.

departments need to be separate and autonomous. So let's look at some of the perceived benefits they argue to make that case, and then I will the present some of the challenges they create:

Benefits of Departmental Separation

Job function clarity is enhanced: Clearly delineating roles and responsibilities fosters a deeper understanding of individual and team contributions within the organization. This clarity reduces ambiguity and ensures each role aligns with organizational objectives.

People are more aware of and clear about their department's roles: Establishing clear swim lanes and ownership creates accountability across departments. It ensures duties are well-defined, minimizing overlap, and enhancing operational efficiency.

Financial stewardship is improved: By championing budgetary discipline and financial acumen, departmental separation encourages greater accountability for financial performance. This focus strengthens overall fiscal management.

Communication pathways are more structured: Structured communication frameworks promote effective collaboration and information sharing across the organization, enabling smoother operations, and faster decision making.

Challenges of Departmental Separation

Preserving and enhancing the company brand: Disjointed departments can negatively impact the organization's brand by creating inconsistencies in service delivery and communication. A cohesive approach is essential to maintaining and strengthening the organization's reputation.

Disarray in vendor and supplier management: Decentralized vendor contracting creates enormous difficulties in effectively managing and measuring costs and performance across the entire enterprise. Supply chain must take the lead in creating master service agreements while all departments manage their service line agreements and collaborate in categorization, rationalization, standardization, and optimization.

Disunity among departments and stakeholders: Building cohesion among departments and stakeholders can be difficult when silos create barriers to collaboration and shared goals. Achieving alignment requires ongoing effort and engagement.

Navigating Hidden Agendas: Undisclosed priorities or resistance to change can hinder the organization's ability to implement sustained improvements and achieve success. Addressing these obstacles requires transparency and proactive leadership.

Collaboration and Communication: Keys to Strategic Success

With all of the disparate responsibilities on a single piece of property, it is easy to see that collaboration and communication are absolute necessities. Organizations with poor collaboration often pay for maintenance and repairs for which they are not contractually responsible. For example, according to the contract one of your organization's landlords signed with your Real Estate Department, the landlord, not your organization, is responsible for HVAC in that building. However, that landlord is very happy to learn that your Facilities Department replaced that pesky rooftop unit in their building and is content to not point out that they were not contractually liable for doing so.

This is where there often is a breakdown—unless Real Estate and Facilities have done their job of continually collaborating. Facilities typically has to dig for answers to these issues of responsibility on its own. Often that continual collaboration doesn't happen.

When I go into an organization, one of my top queries is whether there is a defined policy and procedure for managing lease contract owner and tenant obligations. If one exists, another important question is whether the policies and procedures apply to multiple departments. This is crucial for awareness and collaboration.

When you're leasing a property, what is or is not the tenant's responsibilities can be all over the board. There are some common responsibilities but even those vary. Common are the mechanicals and the HVAC, which are generally your biggest expenses. Roofing and related repairs is another big one. Fire, life, and safety are the third one.

The landlord at a minimum should be responsible for the exterior skins of the building. That would be components of structural integrity. Sometimes they try to slide windows to the tenant, but typically they would also own windows, because that's a part of the exterior. The landlord should also own elevators because they are a part of the core structure of the building. HVAC and fire, life, and safety are typically the responsibility of Facilities.

For those reasons and more, collaboration is a critical function in Real Estate. There are three elements in ensuring this back-and-forth:

1. ***Managing Stakeholders***: Real Estate constantly works with internal stakeholders, including facility managers and building occupants, to ensure that real estate needs are met. This includes educating them about how Real Estate functions. Are the internal leaders across the IFM departments aware of areas of obligations? Do IFM departments understand commissioning versus decommissioning? Do they know what their ownership levels are on the Responsible, Accountable, Consulted and Informed (RACI) chart?
2. ***Maintaining Communication***: Effective and clear communication with all stakeholders means regular two-way updates are provided regarding Real Estate projects and activities.
3. ***Managing Data***: This involves collecting, analyzing on real estate assets and operations transforming raw data into actionable insights for making informed decisions and improving performance, which can lead to cost savings and better financial management. Real Estate's technology platform must be compatible with those up and down the IFM enterprise in order to optimize both portfolio and property management. Facilities, Real Estate, Construction, and Supply Chain need to work together, because in IFM each has functional responsibility in different areas when a new property is commissioned, whether that is a new build or a lease.

All of these levels of functional ownership need to go into the RACI chart to articulate who is going to own what throughout this building's life in your organization. Going back to the narrative around commissioning versus decommissioning, things get missed, and those misses can be costly.

I want to take a turn here and address a different kind of miss here. One that is often self-inflicted when an organization takes over a building—that is the inspection. When you buy a house, would you skip having the inspection? Many times you can't do that because, good thing for you, your mortgage company won't let you buy it without one. That is not necessarily the case in our long-term leases.

On the RACI chart, Real Estate should own a building inspection, or an as-built inspection, before anything ever happens with a signature to take over that space. In an astonishing percentage of instances, this does not happen. Why? Because of political pressure, someone in senior leadership says: "This is where we need to be now because the competition in this region is breathing down our necks. Our only chance is in this building. Just get it done."

This is unfortunate, because all the while landlord is chuckling, because they know they have a failing asset that will be your responsibility in the contract. They also know at some point you might have to come back and fight them over it—a fight you might have a difficult time winning.

Sometimes a questionable HVAC system that you are contractually responsible for can be tolerated in negotiations. You can be O.K. with knowing you are responsible for that as long as the landlord gives you a break on the terms substantial enough that you are confident it will be covered if it goes out.

But what about remediation and abatement issues? Mold is a big example. Do you know who is the party responsible for that in the event mold is a result of water intrusion seeping into a cracked foundation or failed window seals? You *must* have that one nailed down right up front. Not knowing the answer to that because you were pressured for time and missed the inspection is not O.K.

If you are constructing or purchasing a building, that is another story. That is a capital investment that your organization is going to own as a physical asset. The involvement of Finance/Accounting in planning and execution will be vital, because that's not an operational expense—it's an owned asset that you can write off and depreciate.

Again, when it comes to responsibility within and outside of the IFM enterprise, we look to RACI.

Coming Back to RACI

A thorough master plan for facilities management incorporates RACI analysis at every turn. It is a physical representation of how collaboration flows throughout the IFM enterprise. If you have a RACI and everyone has signed off on it, the synergy it creates actually results in less talking, less writing, and less meeting, which may sound like a bad thing from a communication point of view, but less is more, because it means less redundancy and less time, and therefore less waste. That's because everyone understands their part in everything.

The RACI schematic comes in handy many times each day, because it instantly answers a lot of different kinds of questions. These are a few examples:

- "Who is responsible for fixing the windows when they fall apart in our medical office building in St. Louis—is it our Facilities/Supply Chain teams or the landlord?"
- "Our metrics are sliding downward on our Equipment Downtime KPI, so we need to meet on it. Who all needs to be invited to that meeting?"
- "I have a question about what Construction does with the furniture they salvage in the decommissioning process

that starts next month on the clinics in Charlotte: Where does it go and who do I need to talk to so I can get some of it?"

Three quick looks at your comprehensive IFM RACI chart could save dozens of emails or phone calls trying to get answers to those three questions.

It is easy to see other good uses for the RACI charts. One that might be obvious is in new employee onboarding for any of the business units/departments in your IFM enterprise. If your RACI system is set up to be user-friendly it's like a big Frequently Asked Questions (FAQ): You can sit a newbie down at a desk for a morning and let them fire questions at your RACI program. It should be able to tell them practically anything they want to about how things work, who does what, and how work flows in your organization.

What? Another Meeting?

For many people I have worked with in my career, the word collaboration means, "Let's bring everybody together and have a meeting." And honestly, some people like to meet—just for the sake of meeting. I'm not one of those people. When I walk into a meeting the first thing I want to see when I sit down is an agenda in front of me—not some political agenda or pet peeve someone has—a real old-school agenda sitting in front of me on paper or being projected on a screen.

The agenda has become a lost art. A good one focuses the participants, gets to the meat of the meeting content quickly, and moves the discussion along. And like a good RACI chart, it tells you who is going to speak, and what subject they are (and are not) responsible for addressing in the meeting.

The next item fundamental to productive, collaborative meetings is minutes. And a good agenda tells you who is publishing those minutes and when they will be making them available to everyone. And *everyone* means not only the people who were present in the meeting but all those who are either Responsible, Accountable, Consulted, or Informed on the RACI chart as it relates to the content discussed in the meeting.

Keeping Lines of Communication Open

Most people will insist they have an open door policy for communication, but many of them do a very poor job of putting it into practice. A majority of communication seems to happen when something is wrong, but when you communicate in advance that something is going right, you're establishing yourself as trustworthy partner. That means that people will come to you and knock on your open door and say, "I've got a feeling that something is about to go wrong and here is what I think we need to do about it to keep things from going off the rails," as opposed to being afraid to tell you about an impending calamity until it's too late.

When someone is doing a good job, tell them so: "We delivered on time!" or "You really went the extra mile on that job." This not only helps morale, but when that person knows they are not doing so well on the next job and needs some help, they will come to you. This is in part because they know they have some good will built up with you and they can afford to cash some of that in when things go awry. Many managers don't take the time to do this because they are too busy, but a few seconds of good will can help avoid hours of rework and fighting fires.

Education: A Key to Forming IFM Cohesion

I have touched on this before in several chapters, but education is an important part of every department's job of keeping their other IFM partners Consulted and Informed. We see it in Supply Chain demonstrating to other units how to write a solid master service agreement or conduct meaningful rationalization of suppliers and vendors. We see it in Real Estate/Construction explaining the concepts of commissioning and decommissioning and their impacts in the work and the contracting that happens throughout the IFM enterprise.

Education is a critical component in creating a shared language or vocabulary, defining shared goals, and encouraging clear communication channels throughout the organization.

Conclusion

Beyond RACI and education, some of the most important collaborative tools we have are the apps and programs we use every day to do our work—whatever IFM business unit we work in. But many people don't see the technologies they employ every day to get work done as being collaborative tools. Part of the problem is that often those apps and programs either don't talk to one another or the users of these systems don't understand how they can be made to communicate data back and forth.

In Chapter 8 we will explore how to leverage project management software, communication apps, and other tools that facilitate information sharing and teamwork. We will examine how we can use data and analytics to inform decisions, ensuring that our facility management practices are data-driven and effective.

Chapter 8

Integrating Technology into Business Units: The Next Move Toward IFM Utopia

You can have data without information, but you cannot have information without data.

–Daniel Keys Moran

Technology is rapidly modernizing facilities management in a way that does not tolerate the disunity and disarray that has plagued our collective disciplines in the past. This means that how we manage and use data can be the central bond that keeps the integrated facilities management (IFM) marriage together. In the pursuit of tearing down departmental silos in facilities management, one organizational entity that is emerging as a key player that we all increasingly need to help

DOI: 10.4324/9781003773955-9

us enhance our ability to collaborate and communicate—the information technology (IT) Department.

Although it is usually considered outside of the IFM ecosystem, an IT department is doing its job when it effectively manages data, cybersecurity and technology-associated risk, and reviews and keeps on top of each business unit's technology. This department helps facilitate internal collaboration by minimizing duplication of technological platforms and efforts to ensure efficient and effective data quality and flow, end user training, and vendor program management.

With the amount of technological platforms available to the various business units in an IFM enterprise, that's a tall order.

When I worked at JLL, we used a wide array of enterprise systems to manage different aspects of our operations. For supply chain spend management, we relied on Jaggaer (formerly SciQuest). Risk management was handled separately through two platforms—ISNetworld and Avetta—both used for contractor and supplier credentialing, with overlapping capabilities in vetting and managing third-party risk.

Facilities operations were managed through our internal computerized maintenance management system (CMMS) system, *Corrigo*, which was later acquired by JLL Work Dynamics Technologies. Financial operations were supported by *PeopleSoft, Oracle,* and other global financial platforms. On top of that, we had separate ticketing systems outside of Corrigo for service requests, while human resources (HR) and JLL Work Dynamics Technology each maintained their own standalone systems.

This fragmented ecosystem resulted in siloed data and overlapping functionality, making it difficult to maintain data integrity across platforms. As a consequence, the organization often struggled with inconsistent or poor-quality data, which led to questionable analysis and unreliable insights—undermining decision-making and strategic planning.

The result is that you pour so much unnecessary money and management time into these systems, but you're stuck in that reality because there isn't really one singular out of the box solution. And I'm not saying that there should be a comprehensive overall solution, because there are too many variables. In my JLL example, one example of a significant variable is that we were huge and global, so it was difficult to avoid. And truth be told, there are a number of very good applications out there, including those I mentioned, and organizations need to find the best fit for their size, scope, industry, and other factors.

Before I start addressing solutions and get too far into the weeds here (which I will try not to do), I want to make it clear that I didn't grow up as a techno nerd. When I was going to college the internet was just coming to the forefront. Still, I didn't go to school for technology, and I was still a novice. I hardly knew how to use Excel. It was all intimidating for me at best, but when I was at Virginia Tech, my first job before the hospital, I had to manage their day-to-day operations, and that meant I always had a big stack of paperwork on my desk.

Back then I had hair, and I was constantly on the verge of pulling it out. I was always thinking: *"This is broke. Somebody needs to make this work better."* One day, in the midst of all that, I walked up to the lectern at Virginia Tech and stood there like I was my professor, and looking out over all those empty seats I had an epiphany: *"There is a way to do this. I can align every one of these rows of seats, put it in Excel and highlight the color based on where a screw fell out, or the fabric got ripped or this or that."* I could solve this with the help of technology. It wasn't that I was super smart, or the technology was all that evolved at that point, I just grabbed it out of the air, and I thought, *"What else can I learn?"*

So I taught myself the advantage of technology, and that transformed every job. It wasn't groundbreaking or profound, but an intense interest in technology that began in that moment eventually blossomed into aptitude. You might say it sat on my shoulder through everything I needed to solve and followed me into my career of transforming the facilities, HR, IT, and global supply chain positions I held.

Way back in 2004 I wrote a piece in *Healthcare IT News* about the automated business solution we implemented at Carilion Health Systems HR Department. Prior to implementing this system in 2002, which we called HR e-360, Carilion HR received approximately 30,000 paper employment applications per year for patient care, professional and skilled positions. In the first year we were able to eliminate scanning of applications and application duplication, increase HR efficiency, significantly reduce data entry errors, and take the post-to-offer fill time average down from 55 days to 35 days. With the HR e-360 system, we were able to capture applicant data and transmit it electronically among disparate systems of the various HR vendors of the time (Sawyer, 2004).

This is what I have been doing in the 20-plus years since then—creating solutions for automating analysis, weeding out redundancy, and improving data quality and value for sophisticated and analytical applications.

People Can Collaborate When the Systems Communicate

So back to the question: How do we take advantage of all of this good technology we have available in IFM without pulling our hair out? We don't want to throw it all away, but what we do need is a way to make those distinct systems talk with one another—effectively speaking the same language. One way we do this is through data normalization or data cleansing, which is ensuring consistency and accuracy in how data is categorized and classified through a taxonomy. In this process, terms are standardized, redundancies are eliminated, and explicit hierarchies are created. This is needed so we can have confidence that the quality of our data is high, and it is optimized for effective, credible analysis that is so solid that even the people in Finance love it.

Data collection and analysis in an IFM ecosystem involves gathering and examining financial information to gain insights into various spending categories, including accounts payable, real estate, budget-to-actuals, and more, which I detailed in Chapter 3. In this process we create visual representations of data to spot key spending trends, which assists us in developing a gap analysis to find areas where we can optimize spending.

The combination of strong enterprise resource planning and spend management systems allows for real-time data analysis. The goal of conducting such intensive analytics is to transform raw data into actionable, up-to-date insights that drive realized cost savings and better financial management. Such a system should be able to facilitate predictive and prescriptive analytics to forecast future spending patterns.

As I mentioned above, the data must be cleansed to ensure accuracy before analysis, reducing the risk of errors in decision-making. We must also ensure compliance with data-protection regulations during our collection and analysis phases. We should also conduct regular updates and iterations in our data models to improve our ability to adapt to new business scenarios.

I'm not trying to push my own platform here, but I will use it as an example of the mechanisms that are needed to bring disparate systems together. SpendWise and FacilX is basically a spend management system—and there are many out there—which help business people manage all aspects of their spending. In IFM that includes procurement, sourcing, suppliers/vendors, capital planning, budgeting, invoicing, portfolio management, maintenance, and anywhere else you spend money. They also help with compliance, and of course, reporting and analytics.

A good spend management application will do all of the above, but a really capable one is essentially a combination of a *middleware integrator*, *data swamp*, and a *data lake*. The *middleware integrator* piece serves as a layer that bridges all of these different systems and applications you are using by enabling data exchange and communication among all of them. A *data swamp* is a central repository that stores vast amounts of raw, unstructured data from diverse sources without organization or governance. In contrast, a *data lake* also collects data in one place, but it is structured, cleansed, and normalized—making it ready for analysis through established querying and data processing methods.

This functionality enables me to aggregate and present data from a wide range of systems. Whether the source is a CMMS, a risk-management platform, or multiple accounts payable systems, the tool ingests the data and standardizes it within the data lake. From there, the application can further refine the data for specific business units. For example, in the Real Estate business unit, the tool adapts the standardized data to align with the terminology and structure unique to Real Estate. This includes linking property records from the Real Estate portfolio to relevant entries in Accounts Payable and Finance, allowing the data to be both interoperable and contextually meaningful.

It's surprising how often there is a disconnect among Real Estate, Construction, Facilities, and Finance. These functions should operate in close alignment—particularly when it comes to understanding what qualifies as capital expenses and ensuring consistency in how financial data is structured and recorded. Each group often has its own systems, processes, and chart of accounts, but they rarely integrate smoothly with Finance.

This misalignment creates a fundamental problem: Trying to reconcile vendor expenses from the Accounts Payable and Finance systems with data from the Real Estate system is often impossible.

Take a simple example. Suppose I want to click on a property—or a group of properties—in the Real Estate system to identify which Facilities or Supply Chain vendors are servicing them. That functionality doesn't exist. Or let's say I want to extract a list of all vendors providing services to specific properties directly from the Finance or Accounts Payable systems. Again, not possible.

Why? Because the systems aren't integrated, and the data isn't normalized. Without that integration and consistency, it's impossible to get a holistic view of enterprise spending by property, by vendor category, or by vendor name.

Also, take into consideration another non-integrated system—the Facilities department CMMS or work order management system. That's another system you need to align to the financials. Many times they aren't maintained or managed correctly, because they're two distinct systems. So if Finance makes a change, it won't be updated in the external systems unless someone who manages it makes those appropriate changes. This is where the middleware integration, data swamp and data lake functionality comes in, and we have just the thing for that.

In an Ecosystem of Unstructured Data Flooding, AI Can Stem the Tide

If data were money, we who work in facilities management would be fabulously wealthy, because we are literally rolling in it. The problem is, we are often unable not to aggregate that bounty of data into a form that can be meaningfully analyzed on an intuitive platform that does not require substantial human effort to manage. So much of it ends up being worthless.

Luckily for us, the IFM data ecosystem is exactly the kind of environment that AI was born to thrive in—floods of unstructured data streaming in from a thousand different directions trying to find the right lake to fill.

There are a number of areas in which adapting AI to facilities management applications is reducing costs, improving asset reliability, and guiding operational efficiencies. Its data-driven analytical power can provide management insights that can lead to more informed decision making. This "mirror" is increasingly operationalized through agentic AI systems such as AleX, which extend platforms like FacilX by acting as digital facilities coordinators—bridging fragmented data, workflows, and tenant needs in real time. Built on a large language model (LLM) architecture, AleX operates as an agentic facilities coordinator—interpreting unstructured inputs, generating actions, and orchestrating CMMS workflows to deliver faster, more transparent outcomes for both operators and tenants.

This is evident in its application to CMMS, in which AI is driving transformation in some of the following areas:

- *Facilitating Predictive Maintenance*: Through AI algorithms, historical data and real-time sensor data can be analyzed together to more accurately predict potential failures in equipment. This can improve the ratio of proactive to reactive maintenance.

- *Generating Work Orders Automatically*: Incorporating AI can also put work orders on the predictive path, automating their generation from sensor notifications, maintenance schedules, and data-driven prediction of impending failures.
- *Enhancing Operational Efficiency*: By reducing manual labor and automating routine tasks, overall efficiency in maintenance operations is improved.
- *Streamlining Asset Management*: AI can help track inventory, optimize asset lifecycles, and identify areas for improvement in asset management practices.

AI: Exposing Hidden Costs and Unlocking Hidden Value

Earlier in this chapter I was addressing the issue of the great number of very good IFM-related systems and applications that are available. I use the word “issues” because, again, this is only a “problem” if you don’t have ways to get these systems talking with one another. AI is one of those ways.

In my work in transforming facilities management I use a number of AI-enabled platforms alongside my internally developed SpendWise, FacilX, and AleX applications, including integrated solutions from partners including ServiceChannel, Johnson Controls, and Sitelink (BIM Digital Twins).

Using these solutions together equipment health can be monitored in real time, anomalies (such as unusual noise patterns) can be detected, and the root cause mechanical issues can be identified—often before failures occur. At the same time, spending behavior and energy usage can be analyzed to reveal inefficiencies and recognize cost-saving opportunities. Unplanned repairs are minimized, asset uptime is improved, and lifecycle value is extended.

Balancing AI with Human Oversight

Before the advent of AI, a majority of the data we had available to make these things happen was just flooding past us with nowhere to go. That's because in the past our people were the ones who were sifting through that data, deciding what data was relevant to what task we were trying to accomplish, and then redirecting it to where it needed to go to do some good. To call it laborious was an extreme understatement.

AI can transform our work, because when we properly deploy it we tell it exactly what we need it to do for us in various areas of our operations, and in turn it sifts through those data streams and redirects them back to us in a flash as useful, intensive analytics. All of that labor and time involved in filtering through data and logs goes away. And AI, especially generative AI (GenAI) can not only filter and summarize information for us, it can generate new content, and can decide if something needs to happen because of this information it has gathered and can act on it immediately (Baskher et al., 2023).

When a disruptive technology such as AI releases our people from considerable time spent on unproductive pursuits our challenge as leaders is to step back a moment and resist our first impulse. Often, that impulse is seeing this as an opportunity for a reduction in force. I believe that instead we should try to develop more productive uses for the time they once spent sifting data.

This goes back to the self-performance key performance indicator (KPI) that I detailed in Chapter 4—that "gearing ratio" of the proportion of wrench turning by internal staff versus outside contractors. We need to maintain our capacity for self-performance, especially in the healthcare industry, where we have that "extra layer" of responsibility, which is the patient's life and well-being. While we would be unwise to not employ the opportunities inherent in AI, we need to balance the use of AI-enabled technology with human oversight, especially when we get into using AI to remotely manage our buildings.

Why? We need to maintain the capacity in real time to choose human judgment over AI reasoning when complex decisions must be made. This is essential in situations such as response to natural disasters, fires, or violent human-caused emergencies, where there is no substitute for human presence on the scene.

In terms of risk management, less wrench turners on scene in an automated building may be acceptable at some level, but having no experienced technical staff in the facility should never be considered as an option. Imagine a patient in critical condition on the way to surgery gets stuck in an elevator during a cyberattack, or there is a fire and the warning and fire suppression systems malfunction. Say there is an active shooter in the facility. Will AI be able to take all the data in and respond effectively and in time? I'm a big believer in artificial intelligence, but I'm not willing to stake lives on it at this point in its evolution.

Beyond extraordinary circumstances, I go back to my KPI of self-performance in day-to-day operations of facilities. If our response to our embrace of an AI-driven management and maintenance platform leads us to make deep cuts in HR, our capacity for self-performance could suffer and our reliance on external vendors could skyrocket. It's great that our predictive maintenance capabilities are now identifying failures before they happen, but what percentage of our new AI-automated work orders go out of the building and what percentage stay inside?

The Role of the IT Department in Organizational Technology

While I am on the personnel aspects of information technology, let's look a little closer at the IT Department. Why should they have a role in the systems that Facilities or Supply Chain or Real Estate use? Well, look no further beyond the obvious—what the acronym IT in the department's name means.

Advanced systems can be beneficial, but they have to be properly managed. If not, you get the proverbial garbage in, garbage out. That is why in my organizational assessments I ask this question of each business unit manager: "Does your department manage its own information systems and applications?" Many times they will proudly tell me, "yes" and they probably don't like the look on my face after they give me that answer.

The term "micromanaging" gets a bad rap in many leadership seminars I have attended, but in information systems it is essential to achieving high return on investment value. Just because you have a tried and true system doesn't mean you get perfect answers out of it. Inconsistencies in data result when systems are managed by different people, and they snowball throughout the system. Why pay all of this money, only to seriously erode your opportunity to be strategic with your data because it's not governed?

Someone has to police it every day, whether it's a CMMS, HRIS, or whatever system we're talking about. Someone has to micromanage IT.

When I think of IFM-wide roles for the IT department, one word comes immediately to mind: "training." The IT department should be in charge to training people in all business units in the systems and applications. The rest of the IT Department roles and responsibilities flow from there, because to be able to train your people they need to know what those systems are and how they tick. That is, how they interact with all of the other applications in the IFM enterprise and then ultimately with Finance and HR.

When Sheri in Supply Chain is taught by her supervisor to use their vendor management platform and Frank in Facilities is taught to use their vendor management platform by his supervisor, the data siloes between departments become cast in concrete, even if Sheri and Frank are using the same application.

Only when people who are technology savvy can step back and see the whole big picture of what is going on with data in the organization can you have true harmony in the IFM marriage. That is why in IFM utopia, the IT department manages the systems and trains the people to understand what clean data is, know that there is a governed process to ensure ongoing clean data is entered into the database resulting in more reliable data governance, and trust in data analysis and output specific to capital planning, asset management, and operational objectives through interdepartmental business systems.

In the concluding chapter I will explore more about current and evolving trends in IFM, including information technology, but as we continue on the theme of improving the IFM marriage, I want to address how much business we keep in-house and how we transform facilities management leadership.

References

Baskher, S., Bruce, D., Lamb, J., & Stein, G. (2023, July 10). Tackling healthcare's biggest burdens with generative AI. *McKinsey*.

www.mckinsey.com/industries/healthcare/our-insights/tackling-healthcares-biggest-burdens-with-generative-ai#/.

Sawyer, S. (2004, September 14). Healthcare HR goes paperless, too. *Healthcare IT News*. www.healthcareitnews.com/news/healthcare-hr-goes-paperless-too.

Chapter 9

Outsourcing Internal Departments in IFM

The other part of outsourcing is this: It simply says where the work can be done outside better than it can be done inside, we should do it.

–Alphonso Jackson

To Outsource or Not to Outsource: So Many Questions

Interest in outsourcing internal departments ebbs and flows: some years it becomes sexier than in others. Market and economic conditions are usually the drivers, and that can be national or regional. But what is the scope of outsourcing in integrated facilities management (IFM)? Typically, it will be just traditional Facilities-related operations, Real Estate and Construction.

 DOI: 10.4324/9781003773955-10

In Real Estate, lease management is quite often outsourced. Some providers out there specialize in real estate, lease, transaction management, brokerage—anything and everything it takes to buy a property, sell a property, and manage the property from a leasing perspective—can all be outsourced as an entire department. With Construction, you can hire a company to do all of your project work.

In those three areas, outsourcing a department's work is common, but not in the rest of the IFM-related areas I have presented here. Take Supply Chain for example: Most companies will not outsource that entire line of business. Instead they will hire an external consultant, like my firm or some of the others out there, and we become an extension of their department. Being an extension of the department means that we're managing contracts to help with their workload, versus the entire department being outsourced. I am not aware of any company that has outsourced everything in Supply Chain.

Human resources (HR) also outsources to other partners to assist them. I guess you could outsource all of your HR. There are companies out there, such as Insperity, that will do everything in HR—payroll, benefits and all HR administration—but outsourcing at that level is not common for large major companies. Typically, complete outsourcing is more common for small-cap, rather than mid-cap, companies.

Pros and Cons of Outsourcing

The major positive aspects of outsourcing include:

- *Workload reduction*: Whoever they hire, many of them do it as a complement, seeking to reduce their internal workload.

- *Gaining new perspectives*: Hiring a good outside consultant means getting a new set of eyes on your operations. This usually results in better outcomes.
- *Keen focus on improvement*: When you bring in an outside expert they're not jaded and are less likely to be distracted or overwhelmed by internal politicking. They're coming in with a focus on making things better, from cost reductions to operational efficiencies, to technology advancements, and more.

The potential negative aspects in outsourcing from my perspective might better be described as self-inflicted wounds. Two of the major cons in my view are:

- *Allowing internal politics into the process*: Outside experts should be isolated from internal politics. Give them the space to employ the expertise they were hired to provide. Without this buffer their work slows down and your anticipated return on investment from the usually expensive outsourcing process can quickly evaporate. Leaders must be mindful of this because outside experts can be seen by some of your people as a threat to their roles or employment, and the reaction to that perceived threat is often to slow the outsider's work down or even sabotage it. I have found this to be surprisingly common.
- *Lack of executive sponsorship*: A better title for this might be lackadaisical executive sponsorship. Top leadership's enthusiasm and commitment to the decision to outsource must be palpable. If I come into an organization and people down in the trenches are saying, "Who's this guy!?" I know I'm in big trouble. They should all know exactly who this guy (or girl) is as a result of robust internal communication, and why the presence here of this person working as an extension of our organization is so important to our goals.

That point about communication brings me to another item—technology—which could either be a pro or a con, depending on how someone looks at it. It's not uncommon for an outsider to bring inside their own technology into their work at a company, rather than using the existing technologies within the organization.

The positive side of this is if they're bringing outside technology in with them, they understand as an expert how to manage that tool or system. They're not just going to arbitrarily bring in systems and applications they are unproven. Typically that is a good thing because the technology is high-quality, and in some cases, as it is with me—the technology may be their own, and it has capabilities the organization has not benefited from in the past. It is typically going to be better than what you have internally.

The downside of that is they're adding a new system, and usually the data is handled differently from what the company is accustomed to, and that data is routed and analyzed differently. So when that company exits, they will usually leave with your data. So for a while you have benefited from a higher level of cohesiveness and more robust analysis, but then when they leave, you're stuck with an internal system that's still not effective, and that has not been improved significantly in the outsourcing process. So that is a con that has to be weighed and evaluated in the decision to proceed with outsourcing.

When you are evaluating this pro and con, you need to determine whether the technology the outside person is bringing is that middleware integrator I introduced in Chapter 8. Is the technology they are using bringing together data from your disparate systems and presenting it in an intuitive, useful fashion, or is it a completely different combination of Real Estate, Facilities, and procurement applications the consultant has cobbled together.

And the big question is: What is the consultant going to leave you with going forward? If it is an analysis of your current data without the ability for you to keep updating it in real time, that means your main takeaway from the consultant is going to be: "Here's your problem."

Obviously, you want more than that for your money. That's where the selection process becomes key.

Selecting and Managing Outsourcing Partners

As with any outsourcing partner, the selection process starts with a request for proposals and a request for information. These two tools are critically important in an environment where many companies are available with a spectrum of offerings, and to understand their individual capacities you need to do your due diligence.

Have they ever done what you're asking of them? Do they have their own internal expertise? How long have their experts been in their jobs or roles? What are they likely to charge you? What is the complete scope of work they are charging you for?

You must be wholly informed on what those fees are. One example of being caught in a bad place is with transition fees. They typically represent a major cost when engaging an outside company—a one-time expense that is added to your annual cost. So, say I come into your organization. My transition—the time it takes to institute my program—will typically last for up to 90 days. That consists of putting people, technology, and templates in place. Depending on the size of the organization that transition cost can range from $100,000 up to $300,000, and that money is in addition to the annual contract.

Although there are exceptions, that is what happens in a normal agreement, so you're looking at a lot of money in year 1. When you're selecting a company, that transition has to be taken into consideration and you need to be clear on what you get for that, and whether you pay it one time in the beginning, or if it is part of your annual costs.

The next thing gets into what your costs going to drive, and that should be value and savings. What is the savings and value trajectory year over year? How are those going to be achieved? That includes not only the projected amount of savings, but how and where they will happen. The vendor must be very clear with you on the "how" of delivering savings. Labor reduction? Contract reduction? Vendor consolidation? They need to articulate the path or playbook that is going to get your organization to those run-rate savings.

The final question that must be asked seems to be overly simple, but it is important: Is there too much or too little in the contract? This is how it is usually couched, but it is the wrong way to approach the heart of the matter. I have seen many contracts that are extensive, but at the same time they are deliberately vague throughout. The reason I'm sharing these points is that a contract should be detailed but also crystal clear. You should never have to go back to a contract unless things go drastically sideways, and if that happens, the more articulate the document is, the better defendable position each side has. That "each side" part is important because these contracts can't be partisan—favoring one party over the other.

That is why some outside vendors want their contracts to be vague. Their belief in the ambiguous contract is if the two parties ever move into the legal arena, it will give the writer of it leverage that allows them to place a spin on what specifically they were hired to do. When you get into the legalese of the contract, the more specific the detail is, the better, because it brightly defines the swim lanes of the company and the outside contractor, and who was in theirs when things went awry. You can't defend something if it isn't spelled out.

Increasing Costs with Expanded Third-Party Partnerships: A Strategic Trade-Off?

Of course, a major issue in your evaluation of whether to go with an outside company is this: Is it cheaper to outsource part of your IFM operation than to do it in-house? The quick answer is that it should always be less expensive to do whatever it is in-house than to outsource it. But often as the adage goes, people "*don't know what they don't know,*" and that's why they believe are not able to cost-effectively handle this piece of their operations in-house. They are forced to seek the minds and means of experts outside of their organization. Frankly, this is usually because the leadership hasn't developed its team to a level that enables the organization to productively internalize expertise. So, to get a short-term win, they see it as easier just to give the keys to someone else and let them determine who they're going to keep and what they will risk.

So can you save money on third party partnerships? Yes. But would you save more money if you just had the right people in the right roles internally? Absolutely. But again, a lot of that requires not just the department, but those that they work with in other departments to strongly unify or the marriage commonly does not come together.

Eyeing the Landscape of Market Players in IFM

In this section I want to provide some insights into the current landscape of IFM providers, but I will leave the names out in the interest of not overselling myself or selling others short.

The market in national and global IFM providers has seen a tsunami-like change that started in the very early 2020s. Much of that change was what I call verbal vaporware—talking about real change versus creating action. In 2024, things started moving. The trend I saw growing most is associated with a label nobody in the business likes having placed on them anymore—being an aggregator.

Aggregators are akin to an Angie's List or the Yellow Pages for facilities management. They're typically set up as cloud-based companies, but they don't own anything. They just hire other local firms to manage for them. The term aggregator leaves a bad taste in their mouth, so they call it something else: integrated facility services—IFS rather than IFM. What they have gravitated to doing is not *management* of properties but providing facilities-related *services*. The only difference in that is the "S," and this ties into where the industry is moving. Keep in mind that the S is only valid if you're a true *service* provider.

Many of these companies that are now moving into "other services." They have become basically aggregators, but only with slight differences. A true aggregator doesn't do anything but find, hire, and then virtually manage those services. But when they try to move into being an integrated facility services provider, they are doing what I call "management-light," where they are handling other services to expand their revenue. They might move into specific lines such as janitorial, landscape, or mechanical—dipping their toes into service areas where they are already imbedded with the client and have some expertise.

Exploring the Differentiators Between Aggregators and Niche Advisory Firms

Aggregators traditionally focus on the world of facilities. They are also seen in construction, but facilities is a sweet spot for them. They differ significantly from what I do as a niche advisory consultant firm. An aggregator is managing the service side, and they don't want to own anything except for finding a company a better deal on services and writing a better contract. They are more about administering contracts than comprehensive vendor management.

One of the key differentiators between choosing an aggregator or a niche advisory firm is this question: Are they going to manage your people, or are they going to provide their own people? This issue goes far back into this book when I was addressing the critical key performance indicator of self-performance. Is it their model of people management to *rebadge*—reducing your in-house workforce by transferring their company's employees to your payroll?

When evaluating what kind of model they would benefit from, facilities management leadership needs to consider the level of self-performance Facilities wants to own. Remember I said that the self-performance level of the Facilities operation in your organization should be at 65% to 70% or higher. Many companies will insist that they are hitting that level of self-performance, but I find many times that is not the case. I know this because all I have to do is pull the accounts payable data, and more questions arise. Why are they hiring so many HVAC companies? What are all of these plumbing companies doing for them?

Technology is another key consideration because technology is the route to identifying where there are opportunities to save, where they're going to manage their workload, and how much work is being assigned to each individual within their organization. And that ties into data quality.

How do they handle capital planning, equipment life cycle, and asset management? Do they have an internal program to really manage those things? All of them should, but how do they manage it? What are some things that they need to tell you that you should already know?

You need to have answers to all of the above differentiators and concerns to make an effective decision. This requires transparency, and transparency equals confidence and trust. So I will provide both the pros and cons of working with a company like mine: the niche IFM adviser.

First the pros:

- *Lower Cost:* A niche IFM adviser offers significantly lower costs compared to large-scale providers and has a keener focus on way to provide measurable value.
- *Staff Retention and Development*: A major emphasis of the niche adviser is promoting enhanced staff competencies and long-term retention. By encouraging a lean operational model, they minimize overhead costs, enabling clients to achieve significant financial savings without compromising service quality.
- *Tailored Solutions*: Unlike larger firms that often rely on standardized packages, the solutions of niche advisers are usually based on thorough assessments to understand the specific challenges and objectives of their clients. This personalized approach ensures that solutions are not only effective but also aligned with the client's strategic goals.
- *Knowledge and Tools Transfer*: The niche IFM adviser typically does not embed themselves in an organization for an inordinate amount of time, but instead leaves behind valuable resources such as playbooks, technology, analytics, and training frameworks.

- *Neutral Vendor Management*: Niche providers tend to take a vendor-neutral stance, ensuring that recommendations are made based on client needs and objectives. This impartiality contrasts with larger firms that may have preferred supplier relationships.

One last note: Another contributing factor to the lower cost structure is the deliberately lean staffing model used to manage the account. Instead of assigning large teams—sometimes 10 or more individuals—the approach mirrors a high-performing, specialized unit, similar to a Navy SEAL team: small in number, but highly effective and focused. When more personnel are assigned to a client account, the total cost to the client increases significantly due to the full-burdened cost per full-time or part-time outsourced employee. This is an area where costs are often obscured within the broader contract pricing, making it harder for clients to see the true impact of overstaffing. By streamlining the account team, not only are operational costs reduced, but efficiency and accountability are also enhanced.

There are also several cons to look out for in choosing niche IFM advisers:

- *Limited Industry-Specific Experience*: Advisers may lack experience managing dispersed client real estate properties within the specific class-of-trade industry.
- *Unproven Strategic Vendor/Supplier Network*: A niche IFM adviser may not have an established and vetted network of strategic vendors/suppliers.
- *Gaps in Expertise*: Niche IFM advisers may lack proven experience in managing, implementing, and training staff in key areas such as construction, facilities, financial operations, real estate, and supply chain technologies.

- *Limited Capacity for Scalability*: While often agile and adaptive, smaller niche advisers may face challenges in instantly replicating operations at global scale without strategic local partners or extended ramp-up time. Also, during periods of rapid client growth or urgent crises across multiple regions, clients might encounter delays not typical of larger firms with thousands of personnel on standby.
- *Risk Management Concerns for Some Organizations*: Some organizations—particularly in heavily regulated or high-risk industries—may favor the institutional resilience and insurance capacity of larger firms. Global IFM providers often carry broader compliance certifications, greater legal and financial liabilities coverage, and pre-existing risk management frameworks that satisfy stricter procurement or governance criteria.

Total Cost of Ownership and the Decision to Outsource

The total cost of ownership (TCO) in IFM relates to what have you invested in, and what are you getting a return on. As I have pointed out many times in this book, two of the most significant items in reducing that TCO is who is managing your assets and how you are managing them.

Let's start with the who. When it comes to wrench-turning, if you only farm out 30% to 35% of work in prevention, or problems or breaks that is beyond the capabilities of your staff, you are doing well. But wait: self-performance is a TCO issue.

In self-performance, it looks like this:

- *Direct Costs:* Labor + training + tools + technology + supervision.
- *Indirect Costs:* Recruiting + turnover + downtime.
- *Risk Costs:* Compliance + liability risk.
- *Opportunity Costs:* Delayed optimization or innovation opportunity cost.

So, when I say your people need to provide 65% or more of your repairs and maintenance, I'm not talking about 65% or more of the total number of work orders, because that doesn't say anything about value. What I mean is your Johnny and Susie represent 65% or more of the total cost of doing your repairs and maintenance as you manage your assets.

Looking at self-performance through the lens of TCO gives you guidance on three things: The level of competence you need from your staff, how many people you need, and what you need to be paying them. Remember that I said self-performance should always be less costly than bringing in outside help.

The TCO perspective's formulary says Johnny or Susie will be responsible for these certain types of prevention, or problems, or breaks. Now, we've just saved X amount of dollars because we're not paying an outside company to come in and do the work that we're paying Johnny and Susie to do. And that rate we pay them is an hourly rate for the year. Doing this math is not difficult.

Number two in managing assets is the how. This is where the TCO looks at the asset life cycle. For example we are doing our preventive and routine maintenance internally. We know everything is being done correctly, because we have good, competent people, and you can count on them to perform every task. So that equipment asset should last longer.

The pros in maximizing self-performance are greater control, cultural alignment and potentially lower long-term cost if well-managed. The cons include higher fixed overhead, risk of skills/technology obsolescence, and difficulty in scaling rapidly.

Now let's look at what TCO looks like in third-party contracting:

- *Direct Costs:* Contracted fees + transition costs + vendor management.
- *Indirect Costs:* Hidden markups + service line agreement penalties or change orders.
- *Risk Costs:* Dependency or data ownership risk.
- *Opportunity Costs:* Potential missed internal capability growth.

The pros in outsourcing include quick implementation, wider access to expertise, and flexible staffing and scale. The cons can be less control, potential service fragmentation, and long-term lock-in or cost creep.

Also, if you hire an outside company to run your preventive maintenance program, it will be more expensive than doing it yourself, like anything. The second part of this is you can count on a good percentage of the preventive maintenance tasks that an outside consultant is responsible for never being done at all. So there's a trust factor that you have to take under consideration in judging your outsourcing TCO versus in-house sourcing.

I'm not implying that outside vendors are generally shady, but people are people, and from my experience I know you can count on the reality that 25% to 35% of whatever work is being assigned to the outside is not getting done, especially in preventive maintenance programs. I am saying that with self-performance there is a level of ownership that is not naturally inherent in outside contractors.

Some third-party service providers, particularly those operating under annualized maintenance agreements, may also benefit financially from gross negligence or substandard performance. When preventive maintenance is neglected or performed poorly, it increases the likelihood of equipment failure—leading to unplanned capital projects or major repairs. In these cases, the service provider stands to profit from the very failures they contributed to, either through markups on replacement equipment, added labor from rework, or expanded project scopes. This misalignment of incentives can result in higher costs to the client and long-term risk to operational reliability.

The next chapter is for those of us who choose to maximize self-performance and that requires transformational leadership.

Chapter 10

From Coach to Player: Transforming Facilities Management Leadership

As you may have gathered by everything that has come before in this book, I believe that building a high-performance facilities management team in many organizations requires more than just a few changes here and there. It begs a significant transformation. Not so much in the structure, because the structure is already there as a foundation, whether the organization realizes it or not. The transformation has to come in the leaders themselves.

In facilities management, leaders can't sit on the sidelines. In all of my immersion in the workings of other people's organizations I've never met an effective leader yet who doesn't get into the trenches and understand what happens there. They're not sitting behind a closed door sifting through reports looking for places where people can "do better."

DOI: 10.4324/9781003773955-11

It's about helping and coaching versus asserting authority and delegating tasks. It's about unlocking potential in individuals through a mentoring, "coach to player" relationship.

When I come into an organization, a good portion of my focus is on transforming leadership, and for that six months or year, or whatever, I'm literally in the trenches for 95% of the time. That's something a leader has to do to be trusted. Do I enjoy it? I have to admit I didn't at first. It was a big transition. But I love it now.

It's important to adopt the mindset of being a coach with players you're teaching. This is critical in facilities management because many of your people in this business are operating from a tactical frame of reference rather than thinking strategically. Don't get me wrong, that tactical bent is a blessing, and I will dive into that a little deeper in this chapter. Just as in sports, individual exceptionalism can help a team win, but only combining that with keeping everyone's eyes on the prize will ensure success.

In this chapter I would like to pivot, get out of the way a little to bring in some valuable outside perspective on some of the themes I have covered so far in this book, along with focusing on transforming leadership in integrated facilities management (IFM). As I was nearing completion of the manuscript for this book I interviewed two longtime colleagues of mine to get their thoughts on certain themes and to share their insights on leadership in this realm, particularly through a high-level healthcare lens. Let me introduce these two leaders:

> ***Andrew Thompson***. Andy is COO of Zarmanali Pediatrics. Headquartered in Dallas, this start-up is building a multi-specialty pediatric group providing both primary and urgent care. Prior to his current position,

Andy was the COO of Pediatric Associates, which is the largest pediatric group in the United States, with more than 300 practices across seven states. I worked directly with Andy for two and a half years. Our professional relationship began during my time as a subcontractor supporting Pediatric Associates. We worked together to establish an internal IFM program to enhance the sustainability and efficiency of the organization's facilities management operations. The work involved a number of major organization-wide initiatives, including financial reengineering, staff development, program implementations and technology integration.

David J. Jones. David is currently Regional Market President for CommonSpirit Health, with oversight of nearly 30 hospitals in several states. I met David in 2008 during my tenure at Premier, Inc., where I served as director of product planning. In that role, I managed a $1 billion, 50-category portfolio that included global and U.S. market leaders across the construction, energy, environmental services, and facilities sectors. I also worked closely with a national executive board of 18 senior hospital executives representing some of the largest integrated delivery networks and healthcare systems in the country. Among this accomplished group, David stood out. He and several board members brought practical, day-to-day experience in engineering and construction—an invaluable perspective that deeply enriched our strategic initiatives.

Andy and David bring valuable experience from the strategic point of view, but both have been in the trenches where the tactical work happens. I would like to put that together in this chapter with their help. We start with role clarity and accountability.

Using a Matrix to Create Role Clarity and Accountability

In this book I introduced and refer often to using a role clarity and accountability framework to create alignment and streamline processes among all of the different IFM-related business units. I use the RACI matrix—who is *Responsible*, *Accountable*, *Consulted*, and *Informed* in a process or program. Operating from such a time-tested matrix—whatever you title it or however you define it—is a key example of another theme that threads throughout this book—putting considerable time in on the front end to achieve both time and cost savings on the back end.

David reminded me of a time years ago when we served on a committee together. I was a staff member, and he was a member of the board. This was before Zoom or Teams, and the committee members were mostly CEOs and COOs, all from different parts of the country. I pulled them all together physically in one place and we would, for example, interview vendors who were competing for the opportunity to contract with hundreds of different hospitals. He recalled that we were both highly matrix-driven, spending perhaps 80% of our time working on the metrics, scoring the metrics, and then making sure that everyone was aligned on the goals and knew their roles.

Our work together now continues in different organizations and in the present tech-heavy environment, but the model continues to be relevant.

"Today we are so data-driven," David says. "If you look at our regulatory environment we have hundreds upon hundreds of things that we need to report, so getting everybody on the same page can be tough. That's why sticking to our model is crucial. Steve and I do a fairly good job of setting expectations and responsibilities up front, and making sure we involve all of the stakeholders."

Andy also commented on the use of RACI related to the types of organizations that might most benefit from its use, and gives advice for leaders on ensuring adoption and continued use of the tool.

"The RACI framework can be a powerful tool for organizations that haven't developed a natural or existing core understanding of each individual function, department leader, and how they work together, and what they're responsible for," Andy says. "In my experience, the larger the organization gets, and the more departments you have with separate leaders, the more important such a framework becomes."

Andy also believes also that organizations don't always have the depth of culture that we would all wish to see in our workplaces, and that affects teamwork development. He notes that having such a framework that clearly outlines roles and responsibilities helps the teamwork aspect to come together.

"It's a great tool as a potential for an organization where all of that doesn't flow naturally," according to Andy.

> Unfortunately it's also one that I think folks don't always take the time to fully understand. They may get lost, for example, in the differentiation between *responsible* and *accountable*. We as leaders take the time to help them understand the difference, and that it is not just a box to check, but a tool that that can save them a lot of work on the back end.

He also added a few questions leaders need to ask themselves if they commit to such a tool:

- "Are you actually conducting your communications, your planning, your strategy and your outcomes based on that RACI?"
- "Is it the basis for deciding who gets scheduled for your meetings and how you communicate?"
- "Do you go back to the tool, revisiting and referring to it often when you are working through a process?"

The answers to all those questions must be "yes."

"You need to demonstrate that you have a certain fealty to it—that it's not a one-and-done," Andy says. "Otherwise, like many of the good management tools out there, it will just sit on the shelf and collect dust."

Methods for Driving Alignment and Strategic Vision in Our IFM Tacticians

In this book so far I have touted the importance of getting down in the trenches to help initiate and maintain alignment in IFM. In healthcare getting down in the trenches is often called *rounding*, originating from the proactive patient care approach of regularly visiting patients to ensure their safety, assess their needs, and promote their well-being. This can also work in the same way with our employees, because often by the time they "flip the call light" in their workplace, things have really gotten out of hand.

I asked David about some of the methods he uses for driving alignment from the C-suite down into the departments. David's experience is unique in that he came to healthcare from the hotel industry, and in both workplace environments, rounding is critical for gauging two key organizational survival factors: customer and employee experience.

"Throughout my career, I've always used employee engagement surveys, David says.

> In healthcare, it's all about people, and we do a lot of rounding to get a lot of real-time input. So instead of alignment going from the CEOs to the employees, it's the opposite in our world if you're doing it right. We listen to the employees, listen to the patients, conduct a wide range of surveys, and do rounding in improving employee engagement and patient experience. We take the feedback, and then implement what we hear, and then we develop our long-range plans at a higher level. So it really is bottom up, and I know it works because many of our hospitals get 100% participation from employees. This tells me they know that we're going to do something with the feedback they give us.

Andy says leaders need to constantly convey a consistent message of what the organization's vision is of what they're collectively trying to achieve.

"I think that it's fine to put that message on a wall, or add it to your email signature or something like that, but we are all so distracted, so it's too easy to get mired in the demands of the day to day," he said.

> It can feel to the rank and file that senior execs are bouncing all over the place, and nobody really engages because they believe next week they will be dealing with a totally different direction. So the hardest part of strategy isn't deciding what to do, it's deciding what not to do and sticking with it.

Andy continued:

> Having that absolute consistency in messaging doesn't mean that it doesn't stay current or you don't update it to current circumstances, but you create that vision and constantly reinforce it not only in what you say, but how you behave. You always must be mindful of what behaviors you're promoting, who the people are that you're promoting them to, and whether they are the ones who are contributing most to achieving these aims. Every individual and every department needs to understand what their contribution is toward that broader vision and goal, so we as leaders need to make sure we create an extremely clear line of sight for them.

Breaking Down Silos Through Transparency and Communication

In addition to their verbal and written communications, leaders in IFM also express their cohesiveness across business units by the key performance indicators (KPIs) and metrics they use in their daily work. These measures need to reflect not only process objectives, but also strategic goals.

"We tend to break things up into departments, which is necessary at times, but what you have is misalignment of what those departments' objectives are," Andy said. "If you ask three different people from three different departments that all impact facilities what the goal of the organization is, you often get three different answers. It's fine to have your own internal KPIs and process metrics, but those should only exist in service to whatever the broader goal is. Some of these departments can start to treat other departments as the competition, rather than the external competition that's there.

And so you get to the point where there's hoarding of data or of reports, or they play games on things like that."

Andy gave one recent example of a Real Estate business unit working toward measures that did not support the broader organization's goals:

> Their goal was to bring down the cost of rent per square foot on sites they were finding and signing leases for, but they were ignoring the fact that they were selecting sites that were not located where our target demographic lived.

He said this failure occurred because that critical organizational need was not communicated with Real Estate.

Often, people in the various departments need to be kept on track when it comes to the overall purpose, even in very specific, metric-oriented meetings.

"I think if you look at all the mission statements and all the vision statements, they're all kind of the same," David said. "It's all about making sure we deliver a high level of quality, and we always go back to that. In our world, we all take turns sharing a reflection, or a story in every meeting. Some of it might be faith-based, because of the nature of our organization, some of it not. So with that, we're thinking about the vision at the beginning of the meeting, and then that puts us in that mindset that somebody may have a good idea, but it may conflict with our vision or mission. We actually have mission people that sit on these committees whose job it is to steer us back to our vision, and they do it well. This even helps me by making me think, '*Perhaps I need to adjust a little, Maybe I am going down the wrong path here.*' Maybe we need to adjust that. This tactic of setting those expectations and having that mindset up front really works."

Commenting on the Qualities of a Winning Team

In our discussions, both Andy and David shared some thoughts about what they look for in developing successful teams.

"I've had a lot of fun at this new company, because I've had the opportunity to build my own team," Andy said. "So far, I've had 14 people that I have called out of the blue and said, 'Hey, we're doing this thing. Here's why you want to come...' and fortunately, every one of them has come so far, and that's very humbling."

Andy continued with some of the reasons he invited them:

> Those people look smart and know what they're doing, but that is just table stakes—the basic expectations you should have when choosing a team member. The people that I've brought in are the people are consistently and highly regarded as being good leaders. They are focused on finding talent, growing talent, even if it's promoting talent outside of their own area, and they're focused on working well together with the other teams. These are leaders who believe there are no individual successes. They view this as a shared mission: We're all going to win or we're all going to lose.

Along that line, David noted that there is a lesson for moving forward once the silos start to crumble, and this comes from a different angle—working with people from different facilities that were once competitors and are now under one wing.

"I'm starting to see it becoming more common for a hospital that used to be looked at as a competitor becoming a partner," David said.

> So we have to adapt. We have to make sure when partnering with organizations that were once our competitors that we work together to make the region or the city stronger, not necessarily the individual facility. These days, if you're on your own you will fail.

He said that same could be said of a fractured IFM system: for example, getting the vendor management program together for 30 different hospitals. Instead of all working together on what's best for a city or a region, these "competitors" are working together on what's best for the IFM enterprise to avoid failure.

"It's pretty much the same approach," David says. "We make sure we figure out early what we want, and in a very neutral way we take those metrics—our expectations—and we drive success by making sure they are met from the very beginning."

Again, we are back to that concept of putting in the time in the beginning and bringing everyone together to make sure we achieve integration, efficiencies, and realized cost savings.

Chapter 11

Moving Toward the Future of Integrated Facilities Management

Technology is best when it brings people together.

–Matt Mullenweg

If you didn't skip directly to the end of this book you know much of my focus has been on two major areas—people and technology—and I believe you can't have one without the other. Judging by how many leaders seek to achieve realized savings in facilities management—through reduction in force—there are a good number who would beg to differ with me on that.

There is no doubt that to have a successful and cohesive integrated facilities management (IFM) organization going forward the entire enterprise needs to be technology-savvy. Automation and AI are revolutionizing IFM operations,

DOI: 10.4324/9781003773955-12

forecasting, and decision making. Our equipment, buildings, and operational platforms are getting smarter every day.

And even though I am an all-in technology developer and full-blown gadget geek, in my mind, our people are, and will remain, our most important assets. They need to continue to be smarter than our equipment, buildings, and operational platforms so we can keep our assets effectively serving the missions and bottom lines of our organizations.

Our people need to be lifted up—better trained to manage the high-end technology of the automation that sits on top of the mechanics of the equipment. Our technology will continue to improve, as it should. But our leaders and people in the trenches need to understand how the technology impacts their control of the equipment and its lifecycle.

This means academia must do a far better job than it has done in the past to prepare tomorrow's facility manager. Facilities management done right is a distinct profession, and it needs to be recognized as such. Today it is a higher calling. The professionals being elevated to eventually leading it need to be more self-aware and taught far beyond turning a wrench, but still know how to do that as well.

Still, IFM leaders need to be many things but not all things. For example, they don't need to be experts in finance, but they need to be able to understand and talk the language of Finance. In their role as coaches in the IFM system, total cost of ownership must be not be an abstract concept to them, and they need to be able to mentor it, instilling it in their players. Flipping that around, our Finance people need to talk right back with our Facilities managers in the language of Facilities, Real Estate, Construction, and Supply Chain. Figure 11.1 represents the continuum that IFM leaders in every business unit need to keep in mind when evaluating opportunities in facilities management improvement.

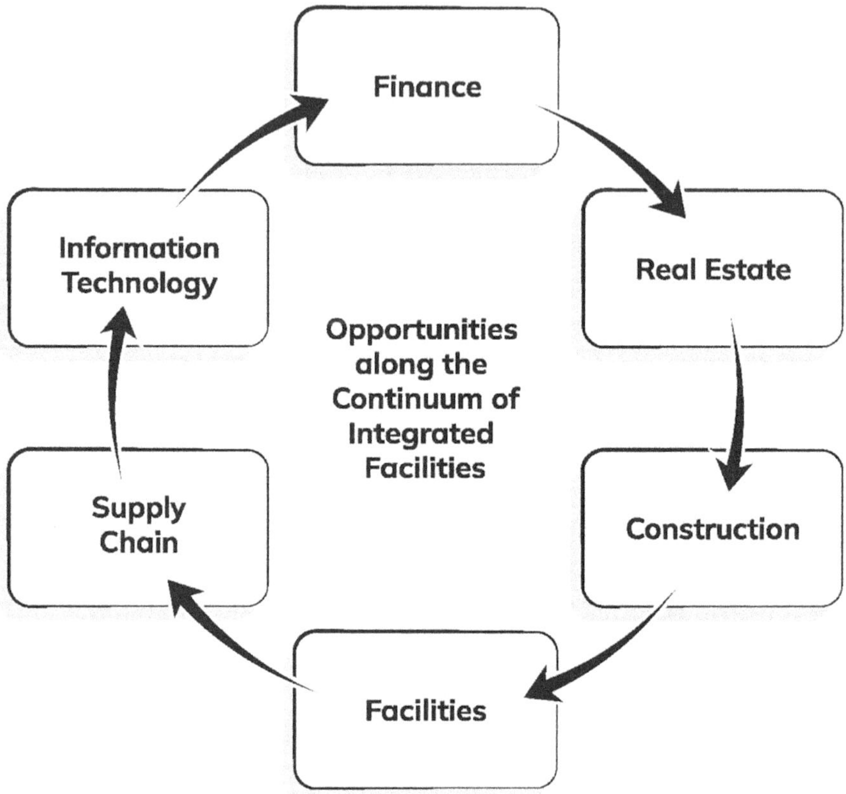

Figure 11.1 A continuum of opportunity in facilities management. (Figure content and concept created by the author.)

Top leadership needs to understand and appreciate the reverse scale of career development. People start from the trenches and work their way up. The higher they go in the organization, the more they need to become a jack of all trades. So, by the time they have risen to a senior vice president in Facilities, they are not just mechanically proficient and technology aware, they are financial astute, they know how to write a contract and enforce it, and they know how to put together and winning team and run it.

Lastly, they need to be a reliable partner, constantly reaching across the aisles—not only within the IFM enterprise but into information technology and human resources as well.

In the future we will increasingly see more highly informed people, because of what technology has automated on their behalf. But there will still be a level of arrogance, and much of that is just people being intently focused on their departmental management, rather than the inclusion and integration of the entire enterprise. Leaders must manage cross-functionally. Technology, in and of itself, can't solve the challenge of siloed disintegration, but it can create a pathway toward solving it.

Solid technological platforms informed by trusted data create a mirror that allows leaders to look at the impact of what they're doing. Using this combination, leaders can provide transparency and empower team members to effectively monitor and manage their internal business unit considerations. Simultaneously, they can effectively collaborate with people in other areas of the IFM enterprise. So always keep your data top of mind when you need a unifier. Personified, you as a leader should be a unifier, but good data can be your superpower in those efforts.

Index

Note: Figures are indicated by *italics*.

For Product Safety Concerns and Information please contact our EU
representative GPSR@taylorandfrancis.com
Taylor & Francis Verlag GmbH, Kaufingerstraße 24, 80331 München, Germany

www.ingramcontent.com/pod-product-compliance
Ingram Content Group UK Ltd.
Pitfield, Milton Keynes, MK11 3LW, UK
UKHW022120190926
475702UK00013B/1554

* 9 7 8 1 0 4 1 3 0 3 2 5 1 *